# The Budding Botanist

## Investigations With Plants

### Principal Authors

Evalyn Hoover
Howard Larimer
Sheryl Mercier
Michael Walsh

### Editors

Ann Wiebe
Betty Cordel

### Life Science Consultant

Dr. Ben Van Wagner

### Illustrator

Sheryl Mercier

### Desktop Publisher

Tracey Lieder

### Contributing Authors and Illustrator

Beverly Tillman
Dave Youngs
Dawn DonDiego

*The Budding Botanist* contains materials developed by the AIMS Education Foundation in cooperation with the Fresno Unified School District.

THE BUDDING BOTANIST                                     © 2005 AIMS Education Foundation

**Education Foundation**

This book contains materials developed by the AIMS Education Foundation in cooperation with the Fresno Unified School District. **AIMS** (**A**ctivities **I**ntegrating **M**athematics and **S**cience) began in 1981 with a grant from the National Science Foundation. The non-profit AIMS Education Foundation publishes hands-on instructional materials (books and the quarterly AIMS Magazine) that integrate curricular disciplines such as mathematics, science, language arts, and social studies. The Foundation sponsors a national program of professional development through which educators may gain both an understanding of the AIMS philosophy and expertise in teaching by integrated, hands-on methods.

Copyright © 1993, 2005 by the AIMS Education Foundation

All rights reserved. No part of this work may be reproduced or transmitted in any form or by any means—graphic, electronic, or mechanical, including photocopying, taping, or information storage/retrieval systems—without written permission of the publisher unless such copying is expressly permitted by federal copyright law. The following are exceptions to the foregoing statements:

- A person or school purchasing this AIMS publication is hereby granted permission to make up to 200 copies of any portion of it, provided these copies will be used for educational purposes and only at that school site.

- An educator providing a professional development workshop is granted permission to make up to 35 copies of student activity sheets or enough to use the lessons one time with one group.

Schools, school districts, and other non-profit educational agencies may purchase duplication rights for one or more books for use at one or more school sites. Contact the AIMS Education Foundation for specific, current information. Address inquiries to Duplication Rights, AIMS Education Foundation, P.O. Box 8120, Fresno, CA 93747-8120.

ISBN 1-881431-40-1

Printed in the United States of America

# Why Are Plants Important?

Plants are the basis of life on the Earth! Plants live almost everywhere in the world. They grow in the cold of the polar regions, the heat and dryness of the desert, in the waters of the oceans, and on the peaks of some mountains. Plants determine what and if animal life will be present in an area.

Plants are beautiful. They produce flowers that give humans pleasure through the senses of sight, smell, and touch. In the process, they carry on their own life and their reason for being (reproduction). Plants are interesting. When you take time to look at them, you can see they have an amazing and intricate structure. They are marvelous at adapting and surviving under very diverse environmental conditions.

In both primitive and industrial societies, people have relied on plants in innumerable—although often unrecognized—ways. Perhaps the most important fact is that people need plants. They have always been surrounded by and dependent on vegetation. Humans foraged for roots, berries, grains, and fruits to eat. They have used herbs, roots, bark, and berries for medicine and healing. Fibers have provided us with clothing. Many of our homes have been made with lumber, thatch, and grasses—all plants.

Even more basically, humans and all other life forms on Earth depend on plant life for survival. Green plants are one form of life that can convert solar energy to food energy. Life requires a constant source of food energy. Earth receives energy from the sun, but solar energy cannot be used directly by human beings and animals. Light energy is converted to chemical energy and is stored in the food made by green plants. Animals eat the plants and we eat animal products as well as the plants themselves. All our food comes from this sunlight-converting activity of green plants.

 © 2005 AIMS Education Foundation

# The Budding Botanist

## Table of Contents

# The Budding Botanist
## Conceptual Overview

This book is concerned with the investigation of seed plants. It was written to provide hands-on activities for students in grades three through six. The major areas of concentration are 1) seeds—their structure, how they grow, their properties, and how they are dispersed and 2) seed plants—their structure, how plant parts work, photosynthesis, and development of seeds and fruit. The last section is a short look at the structure of cells.

The following is a list of the major concepts covered in this book:

- Plants are the basis of life on Earth; human and animal life on Earth depend on plants as an energy source.

- Plants have structures— flowers, leaves, roots, and stems. These structures do specific things to help plants live, grow, and reproduce as the plants interact with their surroundings.

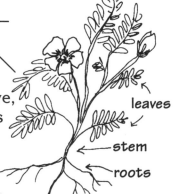

leaves

stem

roots

- There are two main groups of seed plants: the gymnosperms, those that produce seeds in a cone; and the angiosperms, those flowering plants that develop seeds in the fruit formed from the flower.

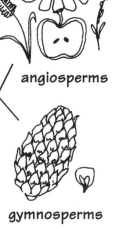

angiosperms

gymnosperms

- A seed contains a tiny, partly developed young plant, surrounded by a stored food supply and protected by a seed coat. In order to germinate, a seed needs water, sunlight, warmth, and air.

water

air

sunlight & warmth

cells

- The cell is the basic unit of life. It is made up of minute structures, each of which plays a vital role in keeping the cell alive and functioning.

The objectives of this book are to help students look at the plant world around them with interest and to build a beginning knowledge of the source of plants, their structures, and their economic importance.

© 2005 AIMS Education Foundation

 **Plants**

are made of cells, the basic unit of life.

produce food by photosynthesis

carbon dioxide  + water $\xrightarrow[\text{chlorophyll}]{\text{sunlight}}$  glucose (sugar) + oxygen + water

 **Seed Plants**

develop from embryo in seed

**Flowering Plants Angiosperms**

**Conifers Gymnosperms**

produce protected seeds in fruits

produce uncovered seeds in cones

Seeds

Seed

dicotyledon | monocotyledon

have structures that help the plant live and grow in its environment

 **Roots**

 **Stem**

 **Leaves**

 **Flowers**

- can store food
- anchor plants
- take in water and minerals

- acts as a transport system for water, nutrients, food
- supports leaves and flowers

- come in many shapes and sizes
- main food-making part of the plant
- can be simple or compound

- reproductive part of the plant
- produces seeds in fruits

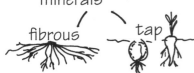 fibrous    tap

© 2005 AIMS Education Foundation

Dear Parents,

Our class will soon begin a unit on plant life. We will be doing many hands-on activities with plants and seeds. We hope that these science lessons will increase the students' interests in the living world around them and they will become aware of the beauty of nature. We trust you will encourage this curiosity at home.

We will be asking the students to carefully collect some leaves, twigs, flowers, and seeds at home. We will encourage them to be selective in gathering the specimens so they will not damage plants and foliage.

Thank you,

_____
Teacher

 © 2005 AIMS Education Foundation

# National Reform Documents

## Project 2061 Benchmarks*

### The Nature of Science
- Scientific investigations may take many different forms, including observing what things are like or what is happening somewhere, collecting specimens for analysis, and doing experiments. Investigations can focus on physical, biological, and social questions.

### The Living Environment
- A great variety of kinds of living things can be sorted into groups in many ways using various features to decide which things belong to which group.
- Features used for grouping depend on the purpose of the grouping.
- All living things are composed of cells, from just one to many millions, whose details usually are visible only through a microscope. Different body tissues and organs are made up of different kinds of cells. The cells in similar tissues and organs in other animals are similar to those in human beings but differ somewhat from cells found in plants.
- Within cells, many of the basic functions of organisms—such as extracting energy from food and getting rid of waste—are carried out. The way in which cells function is similar in all living organisms.
- Microscopes make it possible to see that living things are made mostly of cells. Some organisms are made of a collection of similar cells that benefit from cooperating. Some organisms' cells vary greatly in appearance and perform very different roles in the organism.
- For any particular environment, some kinds of plants and animals survive well, some survive less well, and some cannot survive at all.
- Organisms interact with one another in various ways besides providing food. Many plants depend on animals for carrying their pollen to other plants or for dispersing their seeds.
- Food provides the fuel and the building material for all organisms. Plants use the energy from light to make sugars from carbon dioxide and water. This food can be used immediately or stored for later use. Organisms that eat plants break down the plant structures to produce the materials and energy they need to survive. Then they are consumed by other organisms.
- Some source of "energy" is needed for all organisms to stay alive and grow.
- Over the whole earth, organisms are growing, dying, and decaying, and new organisms are being produced by the old ones.

### Habits of Mind
- Keep records of their investigations and observations and not change the records later.
- Add, subtract, multiply, and divide whole numbers mentally, on paper, and with a calculator.

\* American Association for the Advancement of Science. *Benchmarks for Science Literacy*. Oxford University Press. New York. 1993.

© 2005 AIMS Education Foundation

# NRC Standards*

## Science as Inquiry

- Employ simple equipment and tools to gather data and extend the senses.
- Use appropriate tools and techniques to gather, analyze, and interpret data.
- Scientists use different kinds of investigations depending on the questions they are trying to answer. Types of investigations include describing objects, events, and organisms; classifying them; and doing a fair test (experimenting).
- Simple instruments, such as magnifiers, thermometers, and rulers, provide more information than scientists obtain using only their senses.

## Physical Science

- Objects have many observable properties, including size, weight, shape, color, temperature, and the ability to react with other substances. Those properties can be measured using tools, such as rulers, balances, and thermometers.

## Life Science

- Organisms have basic needs. For example, animals need air, water and food; plants require air, water, nutrients, and light. Organisms can survive only in environments in which their needs can be met. The world has many different environments, and distinct environments support the life of different types of organisms.
- Each plant or animal has different structures that serve different functions in growth, survival, and reproduction. For example, humans have distinct body structures for walking, holding, seeing, and talking.
- All organisms are composed of cells—the fundamental unit of life. Most organisms are single cells; other organisms, including humans, are multicellular.
- Cells carry on the many functions needed to sustain life. They grow and divide, thereby producing more cells. This requires that they take in nutrients, which they use to provide energy for the work that cells do and to make the materials that a cell or an organism needs.
- Plants and animals have life cycles that include being born, developing into adults, reproducing, and eventually dying. The details of this life cycle are different for different organisms.
- An organism's patterns of behavior are related to the nature of that organism's environment, including the kinds and numbers of other organisms present, the availability of food and resources, and the physical characteristics of the environment. When the environment changes, some plants and animals survive and reproduce, and others die or move to new locations.
- For ecosystems, the major source of energy is sunlight. Energy entering ecosystems as sunlight is transferred by producers into chemical energy through photosynthesis. That energy then passes from organism to organism in food webs.
- All organisms cause changes in the environment where they live. Some of these changes are detrimental to the organisms or other organisms, whereas others are beneficial.

* National Research Council. *National Science Education Standards.* National Academy Press. Washington D.C. 1996.

# NCTM Standards 2000**

- Develop fluency in adding, subtracting, multiplying, and dividing whole numbers
- Recognize geometric shapes and structures in the environment and specify their location
- Understand such attributes as length, area, weight, volume, and size of angle and select the appropriate type of unit for measuring each attribute
- Select and apply appropriate standard units and tools to measure length, area, volume, weight, time, temperature, and the size of angles
- Collect data using observations, surveys, and experiments
- Represent data using tables and graphs such as line plots, bar graphs, and line graphs

** Reprinted with permission from *Principles and Standards for School Mathematics,* 2000 by the National Council of Teachers of Mathematics. All rights reserved.

# I Hear and I Forget,

## I See and
##     I Remember,

## I Do
##    and I
## Understand.

*Chinese Proverb*

 © 2005 AIMS Education Foundation

# EXTROSCAPE

## Topic
Plant patterns and structure

## Key Question
What do you observe about the patterns and structure of a plant?

## Learning Goal
Students will observe the patterns and structure of a plant in its environment using their eyes and hand lenses or microscopes.

## Guiding Documents
*Project 2061 Benchmarks*
- *Scientific investigations may take many different forms, including observing what things are like or what is happening somewhere, collecting specimens for analysis, and doing experiments. Investigations can focus on physical, biological, and social questions.*
- *Keep records of their investigations and observations and not change the records later.*

*NRC Standard*
- *Each plant or animal has different structures that serve different functions in growth, survival, and reproduction. For example, humans have distinct body structures for walking, holding, seeing, and talking.*

*NCTM Standards 2000\**
- *Select and apply appropriate standard units and tools to measure length, area, volume, weight, time, temperature, and the size of angles*
- *Recognize geometric shapes and structures in the environment and specify their location*

## Math
Measurement
    length
Geometry
    2-D and 3-D shapes

## Science
Life science
    plant structure

## Integrated Processes
Observing
Collecting and recording data
Comparing and contrasting

## Materials
*For each group:*
    120-cm piece of string
    trowel or other digging tool
    several hand lenses or
        a microscope

## Background Information
A great way to begin a unit on the study of plants is to take the students on a nature walk or plant safari. If your school is located near a park, a brisk walk is a treat to the "hunters" of knowledge. A park is not necessary if your school has grassy areas. Consider yourself lucky if your schoolyard has weeds, because they are wonderful specimens to study, and you will be doing the custodian a favor when you pluck them from the yard. Plants are interesting when you take time to look at them; you can see they have amazing and intricate structures. They are marvelous at adapting and surviving under very diverse environmental conditions.

Humans and most other life forms on Earth depend on plant life for survival. Green plants are one form of life that can convert solar energy to food energy. Life requires a constant source of food energy. Earth receives energy from the sun, but solar energy cannot be used directly by human beings and animals. Solar energy is converted to chemical energy and is stored in the food made by green plants. All our food comes from this sunlight-converting activity of green plants.

## Management
1. Use this activity as a pre-assessment of students' knowledge before beginning a plant study.
2. If you can't go outside, dig up a shovel full of dirt and grass, and bring it into class. Use a lush area that has different weeds and bugs in it.
3. At the end of this book, return to this activity and assess how much the students have learned.
4. Students can work in groups of two to four.

## Procedure
1. Review the four basic parts of seed plants with students. Seed plants usually have four sets of parts: roots, stems, leaves, and flowers.
2. Give each group of students a string and a digging tool and each student a hand lens and the first recording sheet.
3. Assign each group to lay out one 30 cm x 30 cm area of the school playground. Use the string to mark the boundaries.

                    © 2005 AIMS Education Foundation

4. Tell the students to carefully look around their areas and their environment (near trees, blacktop, buildings, or in the middle of the playing area) and record observations.
5. Instruct each group to pick a plant from their area and dig it up, keeping the roots intact. Continue with observations outside or bring the plants back into the classroom.
6. Have students study their plants with their eyes and hand lenses (or field microscopes). Ask them to draw the plant as well as details of the roots, stems, leaves, and flowers (and/or seeds, if the plant has them).
7. Direct students to draw the geometric shapes they observe in their plants.
8. Distribute the *Plant Profile* sheet. Have students study their plants; think of words to describe the colors, shapes, textures, and smells; and measure parts with the centimeter tape.
9. Bring the class together to share plants and observations or to compare the patterns and structure of the plants they collected.

## Connecting Learning

1. How many plants do you think are in your 30-cm square? Explain how you decided on your answer.
2. Why is it important to observe the environmental area where a plant lives? [It gives you clues about what it needs to survive—how much sunlight, water, etc.]
3. Describe your plant to the class.
4. (Choose the plants from two groups.) How is this group's plant different from that group's plant?
5. Why do you think plants have different parts like roots, stems, and leaves? [They each perform a special job for the plant.]
6. As scientists, what processes did we use today? [observing, comparing and contrasting (It is useful to have a list of science processes displayed.)]
7. What are you wondering now?

## Extensions

1. Have students write a detailed description of their plant from the plant's point of view (first person).
2. Do a population study. How many blades of grass (or weeds) are on the playground? How would you do it? [take a sample]
3. Challenge the groups to identify as many plants as possible in each area.

## Curriculum Correlation
*Art*

Bring in potted plants. Arrange students around the plants. Give them enough time to make detailed pencil or watercolor drawings of the plants. Display their art.

\* Reprinted with permission from *Principles and Standards for School Mathematics,* 2000 by the National Council of Teachers of Mathematics. All rights reserved.

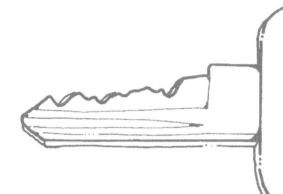

## Key Question

What do you observe about the patterns and structure of a plant?

## Learning Goal

### Students will:

- observe the patterns and structure of a plant in its environment using their eyes and hand lenses or microscopes.

                    © 2005 AIMS Education Foundation

# ENVIROSCAPE

1. Look around you. Describe the environment.

2. Mark out a square on the ground with string. Observe:

3. Pick a small plant to study. Dig it carefully out of the ground. Shake or wash the soil from the roots.

4. Draw or trace your plant. Include roots, stem, leaves, and flowers/seeds.

6. Use a hand lens or a microscope. Draw any geometric shapes you observe.

5. Use a hand lens or microscope. Sketch your observations.

Root          Stem          Leaves          Flowers/Seeds

© 2005 AIMS Education Foundation

# ENVIROSCAPE

## Plant Profile

Study a plant. Brainstorm words and phrases to describe the different parts. Write your ideas below.

|  | Colors | Shapes | Textures | Smells |
|---|---|---|---|---|
| Leaves |  |  |  |  |
| Stem |  |  |  |  |
| Roots |  |  |  |  |
| Flowers/ Seeds |  |  |  |  |
| Other |  |  |  |  |

### Measure and Record

Plant length _____ cm

Plant width _____ cm

Longest root length _____ cm

Longest leaf length _____ cm

Longest leaf width _____ cm

Number of leaves _____ cm

© 2005 AIMS Education Foundation

# ENVIROSCAPE

1. How many plants do you think are in your 30-cm square? Explain how you decided on your answer.

2. Why is it important to observe the environmental area where a plant lives?

3. Describe your plant to the class.

4. How is this group's plant different from that group's plant?

5. Why do you think plants have different parts like roots, stems, and leaves?

6. As scientists, what processes did we use today?

7. What are you wondering now?

# Seed Facts

## Seeds

A seed is a tiny, partly developed young plant, surrounded by a stored food supply and protected by a seed coat.

Approximately 350,000 kinds of plants produce seeds. The seeds of different kinds of plants vary greatly in size. The coconut seed can weigh up to 50 pounds (23 kilograms), while some weeds produce seeds that are so tiny that thousands of them are needed to weigh an ounce (28 grams).

The size of the seed has no relationship to the size of the plant that develops from it. For example, the mustard seed, considered to be among the smallest of the seeds, develops into a large plant.

The number of seeds produced by an individual plant varies according to the size of the seed. Coconut palms produce only a few seeds, but a small weed plant can produce thousands of tiny seeds.

Because seeds must survive a wide range of adverse conditions, they come in many sizes, shapes, colors, and textures. Each seed is specifically adapted to its environmental needs. Likewise, each type of seed has its own requirements for germination. Moisture, temperature, light, and oxygen supply are necessary for the seed to sprout.

## Seed Structure

Seeds develop in the ovary of a plant. Each seed contains a little plant called an embryo. Included in the seed is stored food that helps the tiny plant grow until it can make food of its own.

Differences in seeds are used to classify flowering plants into two large groups. Plants that have seeds with only one seed leaf are called monocotyledons (monocots). Plants with seeds that have two seed leaves are called dicotyledons (dicots).

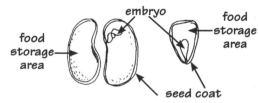

Every seed consists of three main parts, the embryo, stored food, and the seed coat. The seed coat is a protective covering for the developing embryo. It develops from the wall of the ovary. In monocot seeds, a material called endosperm is present. Endosperm is a tissue that contains stored food. Both the endosperm and the embryo are enclosed with the seed coat.

In dicots, the cotyledons are the seed leaves that are attached to the plant embryo. The cotyledons also store food. When the seed begins to grow, one part of the embryo becomes the root of the new plant. Another part becomes the lower stem and the rest becomes the upper stem and leaves.

A bean seed, a dicotyledon, has a tiny embryo tucked between two halves of the seed. These two halves of a bean seed are cotyledons or seed leaves. The cotyledons are filled with stored food. The seed leaves are usually quite different in form from the leaves that develop later. These dicot cotyledons serve as seed leaves and turn green. They last for a short time and actually make food by photosynthesis.

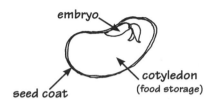

A corn seed, a monocotyledon, has a tiny embryo inside it. However, the seed will not separate into two parts when the seed coat is removed as does a dicot. The food is stored around the embryo and is called the endosperm. There is only one seed leaf (the cotyledon). This is quite thin and is not packed with food nor does it function as a seed leaf.

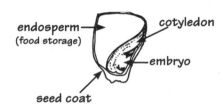

The number of seed leaves present in the seed is only one way to classify monocot and dicot plants. Another way is by counting flower petals and sepals. Dicots have petals and sepals in groups of 4s or 5s or multiples of four or five. Monocots have petals and sepals in groups of 3s, 6s, or multiples of 3. The leaf structure of monocots and dicots is also different. The dicots have net-veined leaves and the monocots have parallel-veined leaves. The roots and stems also have a specific monocot or dicot anatomy.

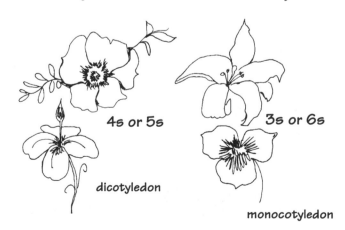

 © 2005 AIMS Education Foundation

## Dispersal

Seeds are usually scattered after the growing season. They lie dormant during the winter. When dormancy is broken and conditions are right, the seeds take in water and begin to grow.

There are many different ways that seeds are spread, such as wind, water, hitch-hiking on animals, and propelled through the air. If all seeds just dropped from the parent plant, there would be too many baby plants competing for water, space, and sunlight in the same area.

Many seeds, such as the winged seeds of the maple or pine trees, are built especially for scattering by wind. The wind currents catch them and the little wings keep the seeds twirling, so they are deposited a distance from the tree. The fluffy parachute, such as the covering of the milkweed, dandelion, or cottonwood, lets the wind carry the lightweight seeds. They can be caught by little currents of wind ensuring that they do not land near the parent plant.

 dandelion
 pine nut

The weight of a seed can be an adaptation for obtaining its necessities of life. As explained above, seeds that are light in weight can use the wind as transportation to new growing areas. Heavy round seeds will tend to roll downhill as a method of dispersal. Those seeds that depend on water for transportation, such as the coconut and cranberry, have air sacs to make them buoyant so they can float down the river.

coconut

Some plants, such as manzanita, elderberry, cherries, dogwood and raspberries, depend on animals for dispersal of their seeds. They have developed brightly colored fruits to attract the birds and other animals. The fruits and seeds are eaten by the birds or animals and the seeds dropped or eliminated as undigested material often many miles away from the parent plant. The animal-carried seeds, such as burrs, beggar ticks, burdock, and nettles, have little hooks that catch on anything that comes near. Vehicles like fabric, fur, and hair give them a free ride to new territory. This type of seed inspired the Velcro inventor.

cocklebur

Some plants forcibly expel their seed; examples are touch-me-nots and lupine. When the pods dry and split open, the seed contents land some distance away from the parent plant.

The main purpose for specialized dispersal adaptations for seeds is to spread the species and to find suitable environmental conditions for growth. There must be adequate food supply, moisture, soil, air, and sunlight for the seeds to develop successfully. Some may not land in areas where germination is even possible; this is the reason most plants produce so many seeds in a lifetime.

pea pod

## Germination

The stages from the swelling of the seed to the emergence of the first leaves is known as germination. All seeds need water, sunlight, and oxygen. A seed contains food needed to keep the tiny plant alive and start the process of germination. The food is either packed around the embryo, as in an endosperm, or stored in special seed leaves, known as cotyledons.

Only a small percentage of the many seeds produced by a plant will survive. Some will fall in the wrong place, such as on rocks or concrete or in dense shade; others will be eaten by birds or animals; still others will rot. The seeds that are eaten by birds or animals are important in nature's food chain because they provide important sustenance for these animals. Those seeds that do survive will, sooner or later, germinate to begin to form new plants.

Seeds are usually scattered after the growing season. They lie dormant during the winter. Dormancy delays germination until conditions become favorable for growth. While the seed is dormant, all its processes are slowed down so that few food resources are wasted, although the embryo is still alive. When dormancy is broken and conditions are right, the seed rapidly takes in water and begins to grow. The root pushes its way out through the seed coat. This anchors the developing seedling and provides a way to obtain water and minerals. The shoot pushes its way to the surface becoming the stem and leaves. Germination is now complete. The young plant can make its own food in its leaves and gather water through its roots.

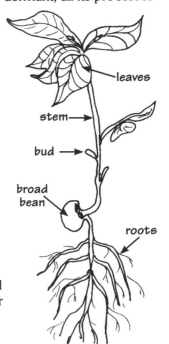
leaves
stem
bud
broad bean
roots

 © 2005 AIMS Education Foundation

## Topic
Observation of seeds

## Key Question
How do the physical characteristics of various seeds compare?

## Learning Goal
Students will compare the physical characteristics of seeds—color, shape, size, texture, and mass.

## Guiding Documents
*Project 2061 Benchmark*
- *A great variety of kinds of living things can be sorted into groups in many ways using various features to decide which things belong to which group.*

*NRC Standard*
- *Objects have many observable properties, including size, weight, shape, color, temperature, and the ability to react with other substances. Those properties can be measured using tools, such as rulers, balances, and thermometers.*

*NCTM Standard 2000\**
- *Select and apply appropriate standard units and tools to measure length, area, volume, weight, time, temperature, and the size of angles*

## Math
Measurement
  length
  mass

## Science
Life science
  botany
    seeds

## Integrated Processes
Observing
Collecting and recording data
Comparing and contrasting
Ordering
Sorting

## Materials
*For each group:*
  *Part One: Making a Balance*
  ruler
  90-cm string
  tape
  2 paper clips
  2 small cups
  small washers for balancing

  *Parts Two* and *Three*
  variety of seeds:
    white—lima, orange, white bean, tomato
    yellow—cantaloupe, corn, cucumber, pepper
    beige—garbanzo bean, squash
    red—kidney bean, red lentil
    brown—grape, beets, apple, wheat, caraway
    black—sunflower, black bean, sage, onion, leek
    green—pea, okra
  small cups
  small bags
  gram masses or centicubes
  glue
  metric ruler

## Background Information (also see *Seed Facts*)
A seed is a tiny, partly developed young plant, surrounded by a stored food supply and protected by a seed coat.

Seeds are produced by plants for the purpose of reproducing themselves. They form in flowers and are dispersed by many different methods. Because seeds must survive a wide range of adverse conditions, they come in many sizes, shapes, colors, and textures.

The mass of a seed can be an adaptation for obtaining the necessities of life. For example, seeds that are light in weight can use the wind as transportation to new growing areas that have proper conditions for germination. Heavy round seeds will tend to roll down hill as a method of dispersal. Seeds that depend on water for transportation have air sacs to make them buoyant. The seeds that depend on animals for dispersal have developed bright colors to attract them or barbs and hooks that latch onto fur and clothing.

The size of the seed has no relationship to the size of the plant that develops from it.

## Management

1. Many kinds, colors, and sizes of seeds are available. Ask students to save, clean, and dry seeds from fruits and vegetables at home. Check with grocery stores, hardware stores, or nurseries for discounted (or free) seeds at the end of the planting season. Birdseed can be added if there are plenty of larger and differently-colored seeds in the mixture.
2. For comparing and measuring, prepare small cups with a variety of larger seeds. For sorting, place seeds of varying sizes and colors in small bags.
3. It will take about 45 minutes for each group of four to construct a balance.

## Procedure

*Part One: Making a Balance*

1. Brainstorm with students where seeds can be found for this activity. Suggest some of the common fruits and vegetables the students eat that have seeds (tomatoes, peppers, melons, cucumbers, grapes, peaches, oranges, and apples). Remind them that flowers in their yards also have seeds. Ask them to gather, clean, and dry seeds and bring them to school.

cocklebur

2. Give each group the *Making a Balance* sheet and have them follow the directions.
3. Show students how to equalize the balance by tapping small objects to the side that is high, or moving the top center string a bit right or left.
4. Let students practice by measuring small objects (pennies, pins, paper clips, erasers, etc.).

*Part Two: Observations*
*Observe and Describe*

1. Discuss the characteristics of seeds with students and help them arrive at the properties listed on the activity sheet: color, shape, size, and texture.
2. Distribute *Part Two* and a small cup of mixed seeds to each group. Have them choose one property (rule) and sort the seeds according to that property.
3. Direct each student to choose one seed from the cup to observe.

4. Have each student draw the seed and record its color, shape, size, and texture.
5. Tell students to describe and discuss their seeds with others in their group.
6. Instruct each student to write a narrative description of the seed on the back of the paper, in enough detail so that someone else can draw the seed or pick it out of a pile.

*Compare and Order*

1. Have students each pick four different seeds from the cup and order them by one property—lightest to heaviest mass, smallest to largest size, or lightest to darkest color.
2. Tell each student to record his or her rule and either glue or draw the seeds on the sheet.

*Measure*

1. Ask students to pick one of the larger seeds and measure its length and width in centimeters.
2. Have each student pick three different large seeds and find out how many of each type of seed, placed end-to-end, measures 1 cm, 5 cm, and 10 cm.
3. Turn the class's attention to measuring mass. After groups have gathered their balances and gram masses, have them find how many small seeds are needed to balance one large seed.
4. Instruct students to make a table and record how many seeds are needed to balance 1 gram, 5 grams, and 10 grams. Column headings should include *Number of Seeds* and *Mass*.

*Part Three: Sorting*

1. Provide students with a bag containing a wide assortment of seeds.
2. Discuss and agree on what are large, medium, and small seeds. Direct students to sort the seeds by size.
3. Talk about and agree on color classification standards. Then have students sort each seed size by color and glue the seeds in the table.

## Connecting Learning

1. What are some of the characteristics of seeds? [shape, color, size, mass, texture]
2. How many different colors, shades, and tints of seeds did you find?
3. In its natural environment, how can the color of a seed make a difference? [Color attracts birds and animals.]
4. If your rule was color, how did you decide how to put the four seeds in order?
5. What did you observe about the sizes of your seeds?
6. Why do you think seeds are found in different sizes? [Plants produce seeds according to inherited characteristics. Seeds disperse differently, depending on size.]
7. Why should we be sure the balance is equalized? [to get an accurate measurement of mass]
8. If you know how many seeds measure 1 cm, in what ways can you find how many seeds measure 5 cm or 10 cm? [You could continue lining up seeds, but it would be easier to multiply the number of seeds equaling 1 cm by five or ten.] Could you do the same thing for mass? [yes]
9. What are you wondering now?

## Extensions

1. Make a seed collection and see how many different species, sizes, shapes, and colors of seeds you can find. Glue each type of seed on a 3"x 5" card. Draw the type of plant that produced the seed, if known. Name, if possible.
2. Use the seeds from the sorting exercise to make a Venn diagram.

## Curriculum Correlation

*Art*

Make a seed mosaic picture. Include a key identifying each kind of seed used by position.

\* Reprinted with permission from *Principles and Standards for School Mathematics,* 2000 by the National Council of Teachers of Mathematics. All rights reserved.

# Seed Search

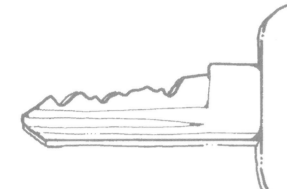

**Key Question**

How do the physical characteristics of various seeds compare?

## Learning Goal

**Students will:**

- compare the physical characteristics of seeds—color, shape, size, texture, and mass.

          © 2005 AIMS Education Foundation

# Seed Search

## Part One

## Making a Balance

**You will need:** 1 ruler
3 pieces of string
2 cups
2 paper clips
tape

20 cm

ruler

### Do this:

1. Cut a piece of string 20 cm long.
   Tape it to the top center of the ruler.

2. Open the paper clips into S shapes
   and tape to the ends of the ruler.

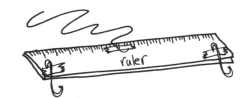

ruler

3. Cut two pieces of string 30 cm long.
   Tape the string to the cups to make handles.

30 cm

4. Loop the handles over the S hooks.
   Hold by the string. Adjust to balance.

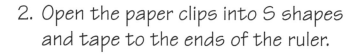

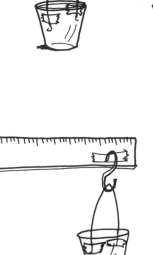

# Seed Search
## Part Two

### Observe and Describe

1. Observe your cup of seeds.

2. Group them according to a property. What is your rule? _____

3. Pick one seed. Draw and describe in detail.

Color: 
Shape: 
Size: 
Texture:

4. Use the back to write a narrative description from your notes.

### Compare and Order

5. Pick four seeds and place in order according to your rule. Glue or draw the seeds. Rule:

1 ☐  2 ☐  3 ☐  4 ☐

### Measure

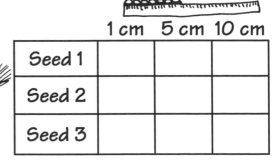

6. Pick a large seed. Measure its length _____ cm and width _____ cm.

7. How many seeds does it take to measure 1 cm? …5 cm? …10 cm?

| | 1 cm | 5 cm | 10 cm |
|---|---|---|---|
| Seed 1 | | | |
| Seed 2 | | | |
| Seed 3 | | | |

8. Use your balance to compare seeds.
   How many small seeds balance a large seed?
   How many seeds balance 1 g? …5 g? …10 g?
   Make a table to record your discoveries.

| Number of Seeds | Mass |
|---|---|
| | |
| | |

# Seed Search

Part Three

Glue or draw.

Find seeds for each category.

|  | White | Yellow | Beige | Red | Brown | Black | Green |
|---|---|---|---|---|---|---|---|
| Large Seeds |  |  |  |  |  |  |  |
| Medium Seeds |  |  |  |  |  |  |  |
| Small Seeds |  |  |  |  |  |  |  |

© 2005 AIMS Education Foundation

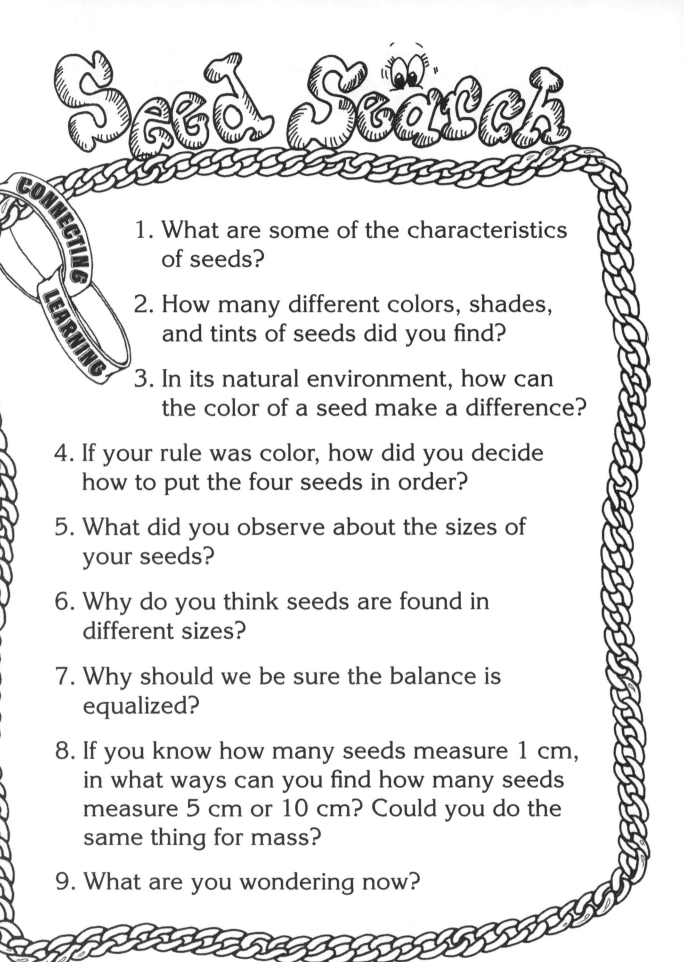

# Seed Search

1. What are some of the characteristics of seeds?

2. How many different colors, shades, and tints of seeds did you find?

3. In its natural environment, how can the color of a seed make a difference?

4. If your rule was color, how did you decide how to put the four seeds in order?

5. What did you observe about the sizes of your seeds?

6. Why do you think seeds are found in different sizes?

7. Why should we be sure the balance is equalized?

8. If you know how many seeds measure 1 cm, in what ways can you find how many seeds measure 5 cm or 10 cm? Could you do the same thing for mass?

9. What are you wondering now?

CONNECTING LEARNING

© 2005 AIMS Education Foundation

# Dissect a Seed

**Topic**
Monocots and dicots

**Key Question**
How do monocot and dicot seeds compare?

**Learning Goals**
Students will:
- dissect and compare a dicotyledon and monocotyledon seed; and
- identify the seed coat, the embryo, and the food for the plant.

**Guiding Documents**
*Project 2061 Benchmark*
- *A great variety of kinds of living things can be sorted into groups in many ways using various features to decide which things belong to which group.*

*NRC Standards*
- *Employ simple equipment and tools to gather data and extend the senses.*
- *Each plant or animal has different structures that serve different functions in growth, survival, and reproduction. For example, humans have distinct body structures for walking, holding, seeing, and talking.*

**Science**
Life science
   botany
      seed dissection

**Integrated Processes**
Observing
Comparing and contrasting
Collecting and recording data

**Materials**
*For each group:*
   hand lens (or microscope)
   seeds (lima, pinto, corn)
   scissors

**Background Information**
   Seeds are alike in some ways. They develop in the ovary of a plant flower. They all contain a little plant called an embryo. All seeds include food that helps the tiny plant grow until it can make food of its own.
   Seeds differ in sizes, shapes, and colors. They may have different parts, depending upon the type of seed. A corn seed, a monocotyledon (monocot), has a tiny embryo inside it. However, the seed will not separate into two parts when the seed coat is removed. The endosperm food is stored around the embryo. There is only one seed leaf (the cotyledon) which is quite thin and not packed with food.
   A bean seed, a dicotyledon (dicot), has a tiny embryo tucked between two halves of the seed. These two halves of a bean seed are cotyledons or seed leaves. The cotyledons are filled with stored food. The seed leaves are usually quite different in form from the leaves that develop later.

| Monocotyledon | Dicotyledon |
|---|---|
|  corn<br>wheat<br>rice<br>grasses<br>barley |  lima beans<br>peanuts<br>almonds<br>peas<br>kidney beans |

**Management**
1. Soak half of the seeds in water overnight.
2. Corn seeds are perhaps the easiest monocot seeds to work with since they are larger than grass seeds.
3. It is easier to cut the corn seeds in half with scissors.
4. Provide a dry bean and corn seed and a soaked bean and corn seed for each student or group of students.

**Procedure**
*Part One: Dicotyledon (Dicot) Seed*
1. Give each student or group of students a dry bean and corn seed and a soaked bean and corn seed.
2. Direct students to look at the exterior of the dry and soaked bean seeds. Have them draw what they see on the *Part One* recording sheet.
3. Tell students to carefully remove the seed coat of the soaked bean. Ask, "Why do you think the seed needs a coat?" [It protects the seed against injury and drying out.]

4. Instruct students to try to remove the seed coat from the dry bean seed. Ask them to describe how the dry seed differs from the wet seed. [It is smaller since the soaked seeds absorbed water.]
5. Have students use their thumbnails to carefully split the seed. Does the seed split naturally into parts? [Yes, there are two cotyledons; therefore, this bean seed belongs to the dicotyledon group.]
6. Suggest students use their hand lenses to locate the embryo (small plant) inside the seed. Have them look for the leaves, stem, and rootstalk of the embryo.
7. Guide students in finding the food storage area (cotyledons).
8. Tell students to draw the inside of the seed including the embryo, cotyledons, and seed coat.
9. Have students write at least five observations about a dicot seed.

**Bean Seed**

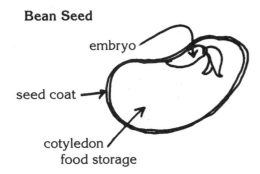

Part Two: Monocotyledon (Monocot) Seed
1. Direct students to look at the exterior of the dry and soaked corn seeds. Have them draw their observations on the *Part Two* recording sheet.
2. Tell students to remove the seed coat from the soaked corn seed and try to split the seed into two parts. (It won't split.) Use scissors to cut it in half lengthwise.
3. Have students use their hand lenses to locate the embryo (small plant) inside the seed.
4. Ask students to draw the inside of the seed including the embryo, endosperm, cotyledon, and seed coat.
5. Instruct students to write at least five observations about a monocot seed.

**Corn Seed**

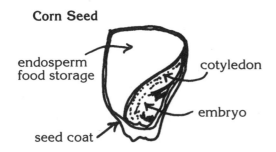

**Connecting Learning**
1. What is the difference between a seed that has been soaked and one that is dry? [usually the soaked seed is larger and the coat is soft and loose]
2. What does the inside of a dicotyledon seed look like?
3. What do you see in both seeds that have been split in two parts? [the embryo of the new plant]
4. What does the inside of a monocotyledon seed look like?
5. Why is there an embryo in every seed?
6. How are dicot and monocot seeds different? [A dicot seed has two seed leaves; the monocot has one seed leaf.]
7. What is the economic importance of seeds?
8. What are you wondering now?

**Extensions**
1. Compare other dicotyledon seeds (peanuts, almonds, peas). Do they look the same? Do they split into two halves?
2. Have students collect seeds from different kinds of fruit. Have them identify each kind of seed as monocot or dicot.
3. Bring in some samples of seeds and have students classify them as monocot or dicot.

**Curriculum Correlation**
*Language Arts*
   As a class, think of ten sentences giving facts about dicotyledon and monocotyledon seeds.

*Art*
   Have students use pictures and make a display of foods that come from dicot seeds and that come from monocot seeds.

                 © 2005 AIMS Education Foundation

# Dissect a Seed

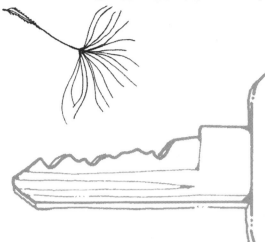

## Learning Goals

*Students will:*

- dissect and compare a dicotyledon and monocotyledon seed; and

- identify the seed coat, the embryo, and the food for the plant.

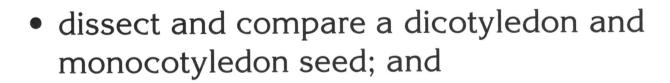

# Dissect a Seed
## Part One
## Dicotyledon Seed

*Make accurate observations.*

*Remove the seed coat carefully.*

## 1. Compare:

| The dry seed coat looks like this. | The soaked seed coat looks like this. | The seed coat looks like this under a magnifier. |
|---|---|---|
|  |  |  |

## 2. Observe and Record:

Split your seed in half. Use a magnifier to help you see the details.

Look for these parts:

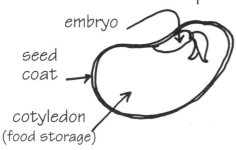

embryo

seed coat

cotyledon (food storage)

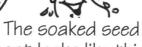

The inside of the dicot seed looks like this.

## 3. Communicate: Write at least five observations of a dicot seed.

# Dissect a Seed Part Two
## Monocotyledon Seed

*Make accurate observations.*

*Remove the seed coat ...efully.*

## 1. Compare:

The dry see... looks like t...

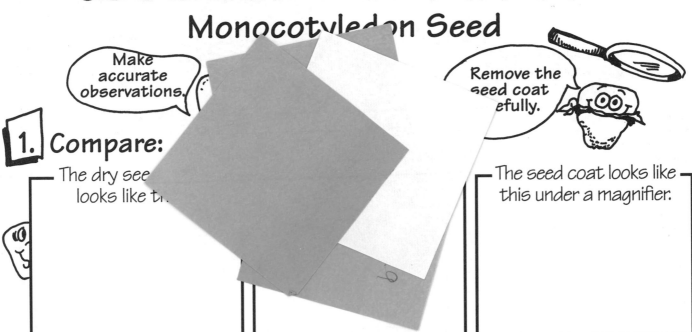

The seed coat looks like this under a magnifier.

## 2. Observe and Record:

Split your seed in half. Use a magnifier to help you see the details.

Look for these parts:

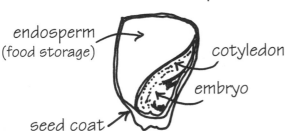

endosperm (food storage)

cotyledon

embryo

seed coat

The inside of the monocot seed looks like this.

## 3. Communicate: Write at least five observations of a monocot seed.

 © 2005 AIMS Education Foundation

# Dissect a Seed

1. What is the difference between a seed that has been soaked and one that is dry?

2. What does the inside of a dicotyledon seed look like?

3. What do you see in both seeds that have been split in two parts?

4. What does the inside of a monocotyledon seed look like?

5. Why is there an embryo in every seed?

6. How are dicot and monocot seeds different?

7. What is the economic importance of seeds?

8. What are you wondering now?

# Seed Scavenger Hunt

## Topic
Seed dispersal

## Key Question
What are some ways that seeds are dispersed?

## Learning Goals
Students will:
- collect and observe seeds,
- identify methods that seeds are dispersed, and
- identify how animals disperse some seeds.

## Guiding Documents
*Project 2061 Benchmark*
- *Organisms interact with one another in various ways besides providing food. Many plants depend on animals for carrying their pollen to other plants or for dispersing their seeds.*

*NRC Standard*
- Use appropriate tools and techniques to gather, analyze, and interpret data.

## Science
Life science
  botany
    seed adaptations

## Integrated Processes
Observing
Comparing and contrasting
Grouping
Relating

## Materials
*For the class:*
  overhead transparency of *Seeds Travel*
  plastic bags to collect seeds
  glue
  card stock copies of *Seedpod Models*

*For each group:*
  hand lens
  seeds:
    water-borne (cranberry, coconut)
    wind-borne (milkweed, thistle, dandelion, goatsbeard)
    animal-carried (beggar-tick, trefoil, burdock, cocklebur)
    propelled (iris, poppy, oxalis)
    winged (maple, pine, ash)
    animal-consumed (cherries, manzanita, elderberry)

## Background Information
After seeds are grown and mature, they become dormant. It is during this time that they are scattered. There are many different ways they are spread around—wind, water, hitchhiking on animals, and propelled. If seeds just drop from the parent plant, there would be too many seedlings competing for water, space, and sunlight.

The main purpose for specialized dispersal adaptations is for the seeds to find other suitable environmental conditions for growth. There must be adequate food supply, moisture, sunlight, and available oxygen for the seeds to develop successfully.

While this activity has students collect and examine seeds that are dispersed in several ways, they will take a closer look at a wind-borne seed from a maple tree.

Trees have a gravity shadow, which is the boundary for objects like seeds that fall straight down from the tree.

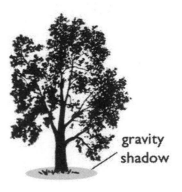

gravity shadow

For the maple seed, the gravity shadow is expanded because the longer the seed is spinning in the air, the further a gust of wind can carry it. The wing also lessens the landing shock on the seed contained in the pod.

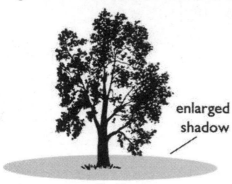

enlarged shadow

Students will make and drop maple seed models. These models will spin as they fall because the air resistance rotates the model around its horizontal axis. The forces due to air resistance balance the model in the vertical position, but the model has enough energy to rotate past the vertical position. The model continues to spin as it falls.

## Management
1. This activity should be done in autumn when seeds are mature.
2. Collect or have students bring seeds or pictures of seeds in each category. A walking field trip to collect seeds is a way to excite students and make them more aware of their surroundings.
3. Make a transparency of *Seeds Travel*.
4. Run the *Seedpod Models* on card stock. To add weight representative of the seed, put a drop of white glue on the black dot in each model. Let dry.

## Procedure
*Part One*
1. If possible, take students on a walking field trip to collect seeds. Encourage them to become familiar with the appearance of seeds and where they can be found.
2. Ask the *Key Question.* Using pictures or actual samples of seeds, ask students how they think each seed is scattered.
3. Display the *Seeds Travel* transparency and discuss adaptations that seeds have made for each type of travel.
4. Have students carefully study the seeds with the hand lens, using *Seeds Travel* to help them identify the adaptation each seed has for dispersal—wind-borne, water-borne, animal-carried, propelled, and animal-consumed.
5. Distribute the observation recording sheet. Have students sort their seeds according to how they are dispersed. Mirror the sorting students are doing on a large chart and display on a bulletin board.
6. Instruct students to sketch and measure the seeds, labeling the part that is adapted for seed dispersal.

*Part Two*
1. Tell students that they will be making models of maple seeds to see how they fall.
2. Distribute a *Seedpod Model* to each student. If you have not put white glue on the black dot, have students do that. The glue needs to dry.
3. Direct students to hold the model above their heads and drop it. Discuss how the maple seed fell. Discuss how the spinning allows the seed to be dispersed outside of the gravity shadow.

## Connecting Learning
1. How many different forms of seed dispersal did you find?
2. What specialized structure allowed the wind to carry the wind-borne seeds?
3. Can some of the lightweight seeds be dispersed by more than one method? Explain. [air and water-borne]
4. What seeds depend on animals to disperse them? [seeds that stick to animal coats and seeds that are consumed and deposited]
5. Why do seeds need to be dispersed? [Seeds need space and less competition.]
6. What are you wondering now?

## Extensions
1. Have students drop card stock rectangles with differing length-to-width ratios to see how they fall. Begin with rectangles that are 5 cm by 9 cm. Have students drop them with the flat surface parallel to the floor and then with the flat surface perpendicular to the floor.
2. On a windy day, have students compare the movement of wind-borne seeds (winged and parachute). Suggest students launch the seeds from about 2 meters above the ground and informally observe the time the seeds take to land and the distance they travel.

## Curriculum Correlation
*Language Arts*
   Tell a story of a wind-blown or animal-carried seed from the time it leaves the pod until it comes to the place where it will put down its roots and grow.

# Seed Scavenger Hunt

## Key Question

What are some ways that seeds are dispersed?

## Learning Goals

### Students will:

- collect and observe seeds,

- identify methods that seeds are dispersed, and

- identify how animals disperse some seeds.

# Seeds Travel

Seeds cannot move by themselves. They must be carried away from the parent plant so they have enough light and space to grow.

## Animal-carried

Some seeds have hooks or hairs that catch on people's clothes or animals' fur. These seeds "hitchhike" a ride far from the parent plant.

cocklebur

foxtail

beggar-tick

tick trefoil

## Water-borne

Some plants that live near water have seeds that float. The seeds drop into the water and float away from the parent plant. Some have spaces inside to help them float. Any seed that floats can be carried by water.

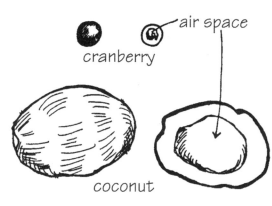

cranberry

air space

coconut

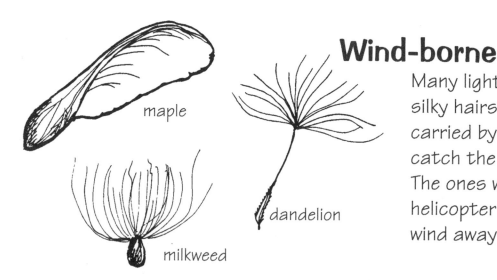

maple

milkweed

dandelion

## Wind-borne

Many light seeds have wings or silky hairs that help them to be carried by the wind. The hairs catch the wind like a parachute. The ones with wings turn like a helicopter as the seeds ride the wind away from the parent plant.

# Seed Scavenger Hunt

How many forms of seed dispersal can you find?
Observe, sketch, and measure.

| Water-borne (floats)  | Wind-borne (winged)  |
|---|---|
| Length _____ cm    Width _____ cm | Length _____ cm    Width _____ cm |
| Animal-carried (barbs)  | Wind-borne (hairs or parachutes) |
| Length _____ cm    Width _____ cm | Length _____ cm    Width _____ cm |
| Propelled  | Animal-consumed (fleshy fruit)  |
| Length _____ cm    Width _____ cm | Length _____ cm    Width _____ cm |

Measure.

0 cm  1  2  3  4  5  6  7  8  9  10

© 2005 AIMS Education Foundation

# Seed Scavenger Hunt

## Seedpod Models

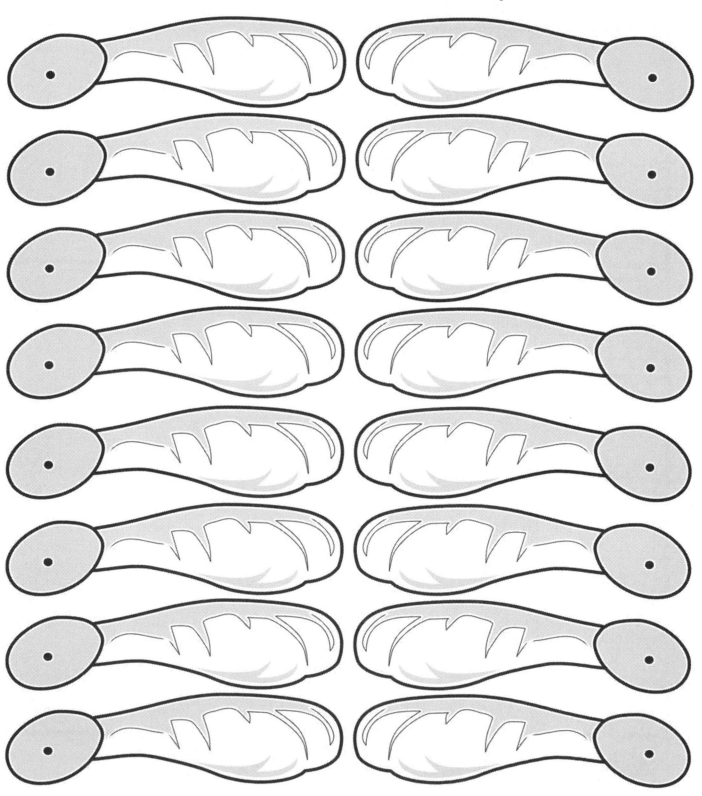

© 2005 AIMS Education Foundation

# Seed Scavenger Hunt

1. How many different forms of seed dispersal did you find?

2. What specialized structure allowed the wind to carry the wind-borne seeds?

3. Can some of the lightweight seeds be dispersed by more than one method? Explain.

4. What seeds depend on animals to disperse them?

5. Why do seeds need to be dispersed?

6. What are you wondering now?

CONNECTING LEARNING

# Germination Study

## Topic
Germination of seeds

## Key Question
What percentage of the planted seeds germinate?

## Learning Goals
Students will:
- plant seeds, and
- observe and record the percent of seeds that germinate.

## Guiding Documents
*Project 2061 Benchmarks*
- *Scientific investigations may take many different forms, including observing what things are like or what is happening somewhere, collecting specimens for analysis, and doing experiments. Investigations can focus on physical, biological, and social questions.*
- *Add, subtract, multiply, and divide whole numbers mentally, on paper, and with a calculator.*

*NRC Standard*
- *Plants and animals have life cycles that include being born, developing into adults, reproducing, and eventually dying. The details of this life cycle are different for different organisms.*

*NCTM Standards 2000\**
- *Develop fluency in adding, subtracting, multiplying, and dividing whole numbers*
- *Collect data using observations, surveys, and experiments*

## Math
Whole number operations
   ratios and percent
Data analysis

## Science
Life science
   botany
      germination rates

## Integrated Processes
Observing
Collecting and recording data
Comparing and contrasting
Interpreting data

## Materials
*For each group:*
   plastic shoeboxes (or a shoebox lined with plastic wrap)
   a variety of seeds, such as carrot, radish, grasses, oats, peppers, sunflower, tomato, peas, melon, cucumber, lettuce, pumpkin
   paper towels
   rulers
   potting soil
   bleach
   craft sticks

## Background Information
Germination is the growing of a seed. All seeds need water, sunlight, and oxygen to start the growth process. The stages from the swelling of the seed to the emergence of the first leaves are known as germination.

During germination, the seed absorbs water, the cells of the embryo start to divide, and eventually the seed coat breaks open. As soon as the seed receives water and warmth, the embryo starts to grow. The root pushes its way out through the seed coat. This anchors the developing seedling and provides a means for obtaining water and minerals.

The shoot (epicotyl) begins to develop and grows upward above the ground. It produces stem growth and the plant's first fully-developed leaves.

Germination is now complete. The young plant can make its own food in its leaves and gather water through it roots.

## Management
1. Beforehand, prepare the seeds and box:
   a. Seeds will germinate faster if they have been soaked in water overnight.
   b. Since seeds often develop mold, soak seeds for about 15 minutes in diluted household bleach (50 mL bleach to 950 mL water).
   c. Line the shoebox with plastic wrap.
2. Use three different kinds of seeds, including at least one monocot and one dicot seed since the growth patterns will be different.
3. Caution the students against overwatering the seeds!

## Procedure

1. Have each group of students choose three or four different seed types (beans, radishes, grass, corn seeds).
2. Fill the shoeboxes with potting soil. Moisten the soil before planting the seeds.
3. Tell the students to plant three or four rows in the shoebox and label each one (using craft sticks) according to the kind of seeds planted.
4. Plant at least six of each kind of seed. Keep each kind of seed in separate rows. Record the seed type and number of seeds planted on the activity sheet.
5. Instruct the students to keep the soil moist but not too wet, and place the box in the sun every day if possible.
6. Have the students keep a log on the growth of the seeds, recording when the seeds were planted and when the first plant of each type germinated.
7. To find the percentage of the seeds that germinated, the students need to divide the number of seeds germinated by the number of seeds planted and multiply by 100 (# of seeds germinated ÷ # of seeds planted x 100). Record the percentages.
8. Have each group report the results of their germination study. Compare.

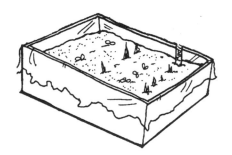

## Connecting Learning

1. Which seed germinated first? Which ones took the longest to germinate?
2. Why is it important for the plant that the root grows first? [The root will bring water to the seed to help it grow.]
3. Do the first leaves look the same in all seeds? [no] Describe them.
4. What do the leaves do for the new plant? [carry on photosynthesis and produce food for the plant]
5. Where did the seed get the food to help it start to grow? [from the cotyledon or endosperm]
6. Did all of the seeds germinate? Did most of them germinate?
7. Did each group have the same percentage of germination in the same types of seeds?
8. Why would it be important for a farmer to know how long it took the seeds to germinate? Why would the farmer want to know the percentage of the seeds that will probably germinate?
9. What are you wondering now?

## Extensions

1. Try planting seeds in different positions (upside down, standing on end, on their sides). Is there a difference in germination time?
2. Grow plants under different physical conditions such as dry or wet, light or dark, warm or cold. Is there a difference in germination time, growth, and percentage of germination?

## Curriculum Correlation

*Language Arts*

1. Write a poem about a little seed that is just peeping above the soil—how it reacts to sunlight, warmth, water, and air.
2. Have the students read the planting directions on the seed packet (enlarge if needed).

\* Reprinted with permission from *Principles and Standards for School Mathematics,* 2000 by the National Council of Teachers of Mathematics. All rights reserved.

| Type of Seed | Date Planted | Date Germinated | Number of Seeds Planted | Number of Seeds Germinated | Percent of Germination |
|---|---|---|---|---|---|
| carrot | 2-13 | 2-20 | 10 | 9 | 90 % |
| radish | 2-13 | 2-16 | 10 | 10 | 100 % |
|  |  |  |  |  | % |
|  |  |  |  |  | % |
|  |  |  |  |  | % |
|  |  |  |  |  | % |

# Germination Study

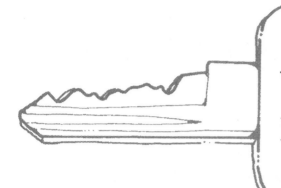

**Key Question**

What percentage of the planted seeds germinate?

## Learning Goals

*Students will:*

- plant seeds, and

- observe and record the percent of seeds that germinate.

# Germination Study

**You will need:** shoe box
plastic wrap
assorted seeds
potting soil

The garden needs sun every day.

**Do this:**

1. Line the shoebox with plastic wrap. Add potting soil.

2. Sort the seeds and plant in rows 2-3 cm below the soil. Keep moist.

3. Observe and record below.

| Type of Seed | Date | | Number of Seeds | | Percent of Germination |
|---|---|---|---|---|---|
| | Planted | Germinated | Planted | Germinated | |
| | | | | | % |
| | | | | | % |
| | | | | | % |
| | | | | | % |
| | | | | | % |
| | | | | | % |

(# of Seeds Germinated ÷ # of Seeds Planted) x 100 = Percent of Germination

# Germination Study

1. Which seed germinated first? Which ones took the longest to germinate?

2. Why is it important for the plant that the root grows first?

3. Do the first leaves look the same in all seeds? Describe them.

4. What do the leaves do for the new plant?

5. Where did the seed get the food to help it start to grow?

6. Did all of the seeds germinate? Did most of them germinate?

7. Did each group have the same percentage of germination in the same types of seeds?

8. Why would it be important for a farmer to know how long it took the seeds to germinate? Why would the farmer want to know the percentage of the seeds that will probably germinate?

9. What are you wondering now?

# TEST a SEED

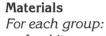

## Topic
Testing seeds

## Key Question
Which seeds contain starch and oil?

## Learning Goal
Students will test seeds and seed products for starch and oil content.

## Guiding Documents
*Project 2061 Benchmark*
- *Some source of "energy" is needed for all organisms to stay alive and grow.*

*NRC Standard*
- *Organisms have basic needs. For example, animals need air, water, and food; plants require air, water, nutrients, and light. Organisms can survive only in environments in which their needs can be met. The world has many different environments, and distinct environments support the life of different types of organisms.*

## Science
Life science
    botany
        seeds

## Integrated Processes
Observing
Collecting and recording data
Comparing and contrasting

## Materials
*For each group:*
    food items with starch and oil
        cornstarch
        sugar cube
        beans
        potato slices
        corn
        raw peanuts or walnuts
        flour
    eyedroppers or squeeze bottles
    paper towels
    tincture of iodine (see *Management 2*)
    salad oil
    brown paper bag
    hand lens
    wax paper (or small portion cups)

## Background Information
Seeds are little packages, each containing a young plant in the form of an embryo and a supply of food for the plant. An important part of a developing monocot seed is the endosperm, which is formed at the time of fertilization. It is the food tissue that surrounds the little plant in the monocot seed. In the dicot seed, the food storage areas are the cotyledons. Starch is the food stored inside some seeds for the young plants that grow from the seeds. All seeds contain either starch, oil, or protein.

The seeds will be tested for starch with diluted iodine. Iodine is normally a tan or reddish-brown color, but when it combines with starch, iodine turns a bluish-black color.

The test for oil in the seeds makes use of an often-observed property of oils—they leave grease spots on paper and clothing. The fat or oil content of a substance can be checked by rubbing it on a piece of a brown paper grocery bag.

Seeds serve as a major source of food for millions of people throughout the world. The seeds of cereal grains are used in making many food products, such as bread, breakfast cereals, and flour.

## Management
1. Soak the bean and corn seeds in water overnight.
2. Tincture of iodine can be purchased at a drugstore. Dilute the iodine (one part iodine to four parts water). **CAUTION: Iodine is poisonous and seriously stains skin and clothes. Do not taste any of the food used in this experiment. Buy iodine tincture that has not been decolorized; iodine should be brown in color.**
3. Cut the potato into small pieces. Place a small amount of flour, cornstarch, salt, and sugar in separate piles on the wax paper or put in small portion cups.

## Procedure
1. Give each student a bean seed and a corn seed. Tell students to look carefully at the seeds with their hand lenses.
2. While they are observing their seeds, distribute the food items, eyedroppers, diluted iodine solution, and paper towels.
3. Instruct students to carefully remove the seed coat of the bean and split it. Remove the seed coat of the corn and cut the seed in half.
4. Have students test the bean and corn seeds for starch by placing a drop or two of the iodine solution on each seed.
5. Explain to students that iodine turns the areas in a seed that contain starch to a bluish-black color. Seeds with no starch do not change the iodine color. What part of the seed turns bluish-black? [the cotyledons and endosperm] Ask them to record answers on the activity sheet.
6. Have students test other seeds and the food items by placing a drop or two of the iodine solution on each. Which item contains starch? Tell them to record on the activity sheet.
7. Distribute a brown paper bag, salad oil, and peanuts to each group of students
8. Have students put a drop of salad oil on the bag and observe what happens.
9. Using their thumbs to crush a peanut, have students rub the small pieces onto the bag. Does the crushed peanut make an oil spot like the salad oil? Tell them to record their answers.

10. Direct students to write a paragraph summarizing their findings in their science journals.

## Connecting Learning
1. What happens when iodine comes into contact with starch? [It turns the areas containing starch a blue-black color.]
2. Which seeds contain starch? [corn and beans] Which seeds contain oil? [nuts]
3. Why is starch or oil important to a seed? [It is the food that helps the seed grow.]
4. What are some other foods that probably contain starch?
5. In what part of the seed is the starch stored? [the cotyledons and endosperm]
6. What are you wondering now?

## Extensions
1. Test other food items, such as salt, bread, sunflower seeds, walnuts, cereal, and potato chips.
2. Test some fruit and flower seeds for starch and oil.
3. Test several different types of paper for starch with iodine. Do all types of paper contain starch? [Remember, wood is used to make paper and wood is a part of a stem.]

## Curriculum Correlation
*Social Studies*
Research the subject of oil from seeds. How many different kinds of seeds can be used to make oil? What other ways, besides in food, can oil from seeds be used?

 © 2005 AIMS Education Foundation

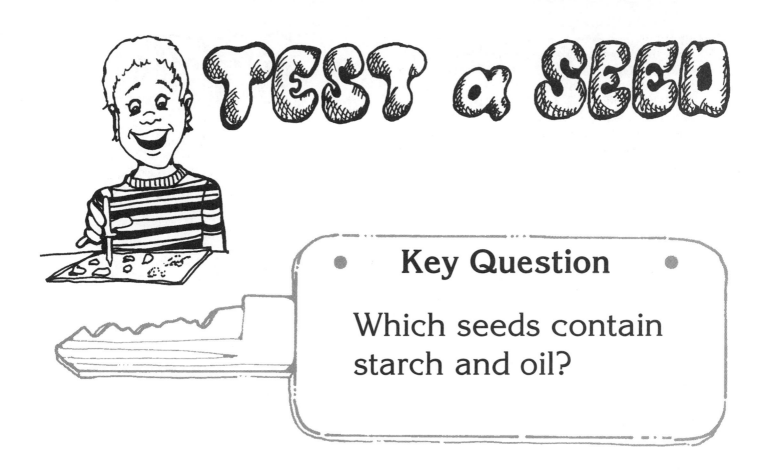

# TEST a SEED

## Key Question

Which seeds contain starch and oil?

## Learning Goal

### Students will:

- test seeds and seed products for starch and oil content.

# TEST a SEED

## Which seeds and seed items do you think contain starch or oil?

### Test, observe, and record.

| Seed or food item | Observations with iodine | Starch? yes/no | Observations crushed on paper bag | Oil? yes/no |
|---|---|---|---|---|
| bean | | | | |
| corn | | | | |
| potato slice | | | | |
| corn starch | | | | |
| flour (wheat) | | | | |
| sugar (beets/cane) | | | | |
| peanut | | | | |
| salad oil | | | | |

Iodine will turn bluish-black if starch is present.

Oil will leave spots on the brown bag.

© 2005 AIMS Education Foundation

# TEST a SEED

**CONNECTING LEARNING**

1. What happens when iodine comes into contact with starch?

2. Which seeds contain starch? Which seeds contain oil?

3. Why is starch or oil important to a seed?

4. What are some other foods that probably contain starch?

5. In what part of the seed is the starch stored?

6. What are you wondering now?

# Exploring Germination

**Topic**
Growing seeds

**Key Question**
What do you observe about seeds when they germinate?

**Learning Goals**
Students will:
- plant a spoonful of mixed seeds, and
- observe the seeds germinating.

**Guiding Documents**
*Project 2061 Benchmarks*
- *A great variety of kinds of living things can be sorted into groups in many ways using various features to decide which things belong to which group.*
- *Over the whole earth, organisms are growing, dying, and decaying, and new organisms are being produced by the old ones.*

*NRC Standard*
- *Plants and animals have life cycles that include being born, developing into adults, reproducing, and eventually dying. The details of this life cycle are different for different organisms.*

**Science**
Life science
    botany
        germination

**Integrated Processes**
Predicting
Observing
Sorting
Collecting and recording data
Comparing and contrasting

**Materials**
*For each group:*
    1 resealable plastic bag
    two-sided tape
    1 tablespoon of birdseed or mixed seeds
        (lima, pinto, grass, corn, radish, mung)
    paper towels
    hand lens

**Background Information**
Germination is the growing of a seed. All seeds need water, sunlight, and oxygen. The stages from the swelling of the seed to the emergence of the first leaves are known as germination. A seed contains food to support the life of the tiny plant. When a seed begins to grow, it takes in water and swells. Usually the root tip emerges out of the seed first. This helps the plant absorb water and anchors the developing seedling. Next, the young stem and leaves emerge from the seed. The leaves turn green when sunlight reaches them and they start to produce their own food by photosynthesis.

**Management**
1. Gather an assortment of seeds. If using birdseed, be sure there are five or six different types of seeds in it. You may also use mixed seeds: lima beans, pinto beans, grass, corn, radish, or mung beans.
2. Seeds are easier to see on two-sided tape. If you must use one-sided tape, put the seeds on the sticky side, turn the tape over, and fasten it to the paper towel.
3. Students should wash their hands before and after handling the seeds. It is easy to transfer mildew onto their hands.
4. If mildew appears inside a bag, dispose of the plastic-bag garden without opening it!

**Procedure**
1. Give each student or group of students the recording sheet *Make a Mini-Garden,* a resealable plastic bag, a spoonful of birdseed or mixed seed, a paper towel, and a long strip of two-sided tape.
2. Direct students to predict the number of seeds they have, then count and sort them by types.
3. Discuss with students the different sizes, shapes, and colors of seeds in their samples. Identify the different types of seeds, if possible.
4. Have students fold the paper towel to fit in the plastic bag, cut a strip of tape for each type of seed, and place the tape on the paper towel in rows.
5. Instruct students to "plant" one seed type in each row and label the rows A, B, C, D, and so on.
6. Have students predict and record which type of seed they think will sprout (germinate) first.
7. Tell students to dampen the paper towel, carefully put the garden in the plastic bag, and seal the bag. Put the bags up on a bulletin board with pins or on a window with tape.

8. Try putting a few of the bags in a dark closet or desk drawer. How well do the seeds grow? Compare the germination of these seeds with those exposed to the light.
9. Instruct students to use hand lenses to watch the growth of the seeds. Does the first growth of each seed look the same? Have students record observations in their *Garden Logs*. [root appeared, stem grew, etc.]

## Connecting Learning

1. How many days did it take for the first seed to germinate?
2. What do seeds need to germinate?
3. Describe how one type of seed germinated.
4. Why is germination important in the life cycle of a plant?
5. What are you wondering now?

## Extension

Have students design experiments to discover what seeds need in order to germinate. Plastic-bag gardens could be placed in sunlight and darkness, in hot and cold temperatures, and with and without water. When the seedlings have grown, transplant them to an outside garden.

## Curriculum Correlation

*Art*

On small pieces of paper (2" x 3"), draw the daily growth of one seedling. After 10 to 20 pictures, staple along one edge to make a flip book about plant growth.

*Language Arts*

The students can write a paragraph about how the mini-garden grew using the information from their *Garden Logs*.

# Exploring Germination

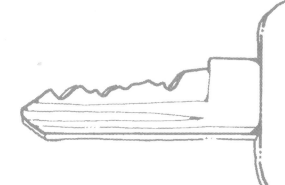

## Key Question

What do you observe about seeds when they germinate?

## Learning Goals

**Students will:**

- plant a spoonful of mixed seeds, and

- observe the seeds germinating.

# Exploring Germination
## Make a **Mini-Garden**

**You will need:** spoonful of mixed seeds
sealable plastic bag
two-sided tape
paper towel
water
sunlight

1. Get a spoonful of seeds.

2. Estimate how many seeds you have: _____ Count them: _____

3. Sort your seeds. How many types are there?

4. Fold the paper towel to fit into the plastic bag. Cut as many pieces of tape as you have types of seeds. Place the tape on the paper towel to make rows.

5. "Plant" one seed type in each row. Label the rows A, B, C, D....

6. Which type of seed do you think will sprout first? _____

7. Wet the paper towel and carefully put your garden in the bag.

## Garden Log

| | |
|---|---|
| Day 1: | Day 6: |
| Day 2: | Day 7: |
| Day 3: | Day 8: |
| Day 4: | Day 9: |
| Day 5: | Day 10: |

8. When your seedlings have grown, transplant them to a real garden.

# Exploring Germination

1. How many days did it take for the first seed to germinate?

2. What do seeds need to germinate?

3. Describe how one type of seed germinated.

4. Why is germination important in the life cycle of a plant?

5. What are you wondering now?

# COMPARING GERMINATION

**Topic**
Germination of monocot and dicot seeds

**Key Question**
How does a monocot plant compare with a dicot plant?

**Learning Goals**
Students will:
• observe the germination of monocots and dicots, and
• compare plant characteristics.

**Guiding Documents**
*Project 2061 Benchmark*
• *Scientific investigations may take many different forms, including observing what things are like or what is happening somewhere, collecting specimens for analysis, and doing experiments. Investigations can focus on physical, biological, and social questions.*

*NRC Standards*
• *Scientists use different kinds of investigations depending on the questions they are trying to answer. Types of investigations include describing objects, events, and organisms; classifying them; and doing a fair test (experimenting).*
• *Employ simple equipment and tools to gather data and extend the senses.*

*NCTM Standards 2000\**
• *Select and apply appropriate standard units and tools to measure length, area, volume, weight, time, temperature, and the size of angles*
• *Represent data using tables and graphs such as line plots, bar graphs, and line graphs*

**Math**
Measurement
    length
Graphing
    bar

**Science**
Life science
    botany
        germination

**Integrated Processes**
Observing
Collecting and recording data
Comparing and contrasting

**Materials**
*For each group:*
    2 dicot seeds: beans, peas
    2 monocot seeds: corn, grasses
    hand lens
    2 transparent containers (or 8-oz plastic cups)
    paper towels
    filler for containers (see *Management 3*)
    tape for two labels
    metric ruler

**Background Information**
Germination is the sprouting of a seed. In nature, seeds normally germinate beneath the soil, making it difficult to observe how they grow. The first growth of a seed during germination is from the lower portion of the embryo which is called the radicle (root). It pushes out through the seed coat and grows downward providing water, minerals, and an anchor for the plant. The epicotyl, the upper part of the embryo, develops into the leaves and upper portions of the stem. The epicotyl grows upward, pushing through the dirt toward light.

Monocot and dicot seeds have observable differences during germination. In both, the root develops first. In a monocot (corn seed), the seed stays under the ground. The single seed leaf is wrapped around the tall, tubelike stem. As the seed grows, the stem and leaf push upward above the ground. The vein structure of a monocot leaf is usually parallel. Monocots include grasses, lilies, irises, and palms.

A dicot seed's (bean) first leaves are the cotyledons that push above the ground as the stem grows. The true leaves develop secondly and grow out from the stem. The vein structure of the leaves is usually netlike. The dicots include many of the familiar trees, shrubs, and flowers.

**Management**
1. It may be important to review the characteristics of monocot and dicot seeds.
2. The seeds will germinate faster if you soak them overnight.
3. Filler used to stuff the middle of the containers may include paper towels, newspaper, cotton, or vermiculite.
4. Divide the class into small groups. Have each group choose an initial or name to identify their plants.

## Procedure

1. Ask *the Key* Question How does a monocot plant compare with a dicot plant? Tell the class that each group will grow two dicot and two monocot seeds and compare the plants that develop.

2. Have each small group gather materials and prepare the containers as follows:
   - Line the inside of each container with a wet, folded paper towel.
   - To hold the wet towel against the side, stuff a paper towel into the middle of each container.
   - Place two soaked dicot seeds between the paper towel and the side of one container. Add a piece of tape labeled with the group's initial and "dicot."
   - Insert two soaked monocot seeds in the second container and label "monocot."
   - Fill the containers with water to just below the lowest seed. The paper towel will soak up the water and keep the seeds moist.

3. Keep the containers in a warm, sunny location and water them carefully. Invite students to observe the seeds as they germinate and grow.

4. After five days, distribute the graph sheet. Have students measure and graph plant growth every fifth day. Direct them to hold a metric ruler (or the graph itself) against the side of the container with the *zero* mark at the level where the seeds are planted.

5. At the same time, give students the *Observation Notes* sheet. Instruct them to draw the plants every fifth day, carefully recording how the roots, first leaves, second leaves, etc., look and when they appear. (see questions in *Connecting Learning.)*

6. After the twentieth day, have students use their observation notes to write a comparison of the monocot plant with the dicot plant—including differences in growth and appearance—on the back of the paper.

7. Guide the class as they compare their observations with each other. Post their graphs and observations on the bulletin board.

## Connecting Learning

1. What part of the new plant is the first to appear from the seed? [root] How long after planting does this happen?
2. When did the first shoot appear?
3. How do the first leaves compare? [The first leaves of a dicot are the plant's cotyledons; the first leaves of a monocot will be thin, narrow, and parallel-veined, capable of carrying on photosynthesis.]
4. For each seed type, how does the second set of leaves compare to the first set?
5. How fast did the seeds grow compared to each other?
6. How are the two types of plants different?
7. What are you wondering now?

## Extensions

1. Germinate other monocot and dicot seeds.
2. Plant seeds in several different positions. How does position affect growth?

* Reprinted with permission from *Principles and Standards for School Mathematics,* 2000 by the National Council of Teachers of Mathematics. All rights reserved.

# Comparing Germination

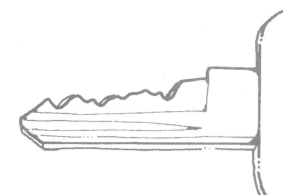

## Key Question

How does a monocot plant compare with a dicot plant?

## Learning Goals

Students will:

- observe the germination of monocots and dicots, and

- compare plant characteristics.

# Comparing Germination

## Dicot Growth

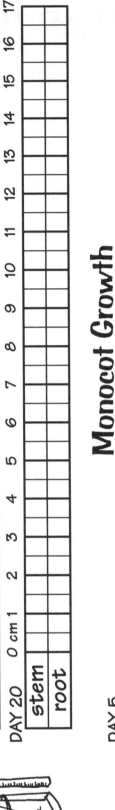

| | 0 cm 1 | 2 | 3 | 4 | 5 | 6 | 7 | 8 | 9 | 10 | 11 | 12 | 13 | 14 | 15 | 16 | 17 |
|---|---|---|---|---|---|---|---|---|---|---|---|---|---|---|---|---|---|
| **DAY 5** stem | | | | | | | | | | | | | | | | | |
| root | | | | | | | | | | | | | | | | | |
| **DAY 10** stem | | | | | | | | | | | | | | | | | |
| root | | | | | | | | | | | | | | | | | |
| **DAY 15** stem | | | | | | | | | | | | | | | | | |
| root | | | | | | | | | | | | | | | | | |
| **DAY 20** stem | | | | | | | | | | | | | | | | | |
| root | | | | | | | | | | | | | | | | | |

## Monocot Growth

| | 0 cm 1 | 2 | 3 | 4 | 5 | 6 | 7 | 8 | 9 | 10 | 11 | 12 | 13 | 14 | 15 | 16 | 17 |
|---|---|---|---|---|---|---|---|---|---|---|---|---|---|---|---|---|---|
| **DAY 5** stem | | | | | | | | | | | | | | | | | |
| root | | | | | | | | | | | | | | | | | |
| **DAY 10** stem | | | | | | | | | | | | | | | | | |
| root | | | | | | | | | | | | | | | | | |
| **DAY 15** stem | | | | | | | | | | | | | | | | | |
| root | | | | | | | | | | | | | | | | | |
| **DAY 20** stem | | | | | | | | | | | | | | | | | |
| root | | | | | | | | | | | | | | | | | |

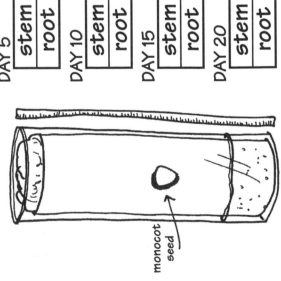

ruler

cotton

tall glass

paper towel

dicot seed

water

monocot seed

© 2005 AIMS Education Foundation

# COMPARING GERMINATION
## Observation Notes

**Day 5**

| | dicot 🫘 | monocot 🌾 |
|---|---|---|
| leaves | | |
| stem | | |
| roots | | |

**Day 10**

| | dicot 🫘 | monocot 🌾 |
|---|---|---|
| leaves | | |
| stem | | |
| roots | | |

**Day 15**

| | dicot 🫘 | monocot 🌾 |
|---|---|---|
| leaves | | |
| stem | | |
| roots | | |

**Day 20**

| | dicot 🫘 | monocot 🌾 |
|---|---|---|
| leaves | | |
| stem | | |
| roots | | |

Write several sentences comparing monocot and dicot plants on the back.

 © 2005 AIMS Education Foundation

# COMPARING GERMINATION

1. What part of the new plant is the first to appear from the seed? How long after planting does this happen?

2. When did the first shoot appear?

3. How do the first leaves compare?

4. For each seed type, how does the second set of leaves compare to the first set?

5. How fast did the seeds grow compared to each other?

6. How are the two types of plants different?

7. What are you wondering now?

# Seed Plants

Over 300,000 kinds of plants produce seeds. These plants bear seeds—in flowers or cones—to reproduce themselves. Seed plants are divided into two main groups: angiosperms and gymnosperms.

*Angiosperms* are plants that produce flowers and fruits. Their seeds have a protective covering, usually fleshy fruit (peaches, cherries, etc.), pods (beans, peas), or a shell (walnuts, pecans, etc.). Most of the plants that produce the fruits, grains, and vegetables that we eat are angiosperms. The seeds come from the ovule and the fruit comes from the ovary of a flower. Angiosperms are further divided into monocot and dicot plants.

*Gymnosperms* are trees and shrubs that produce uncovered seeds. Most gymnosperms bear their seeds in cones. Conifers are the best known gymnosperms. Most conifers have needle-like or scale-like leaves. The pine, fir, spruce, hemlock, and larch are conifers.

## Gymnosperms

Gymnosperms are plants that have naked or uncovered seeds. You will not see flowers growing from a pine tree or a fir tree. The seeds are borne between the scales of the female cone. A cone, the reproductive organ of a conifer, is made up of woody scales that overlap. Two seeds lie on top of one scale and are partly covered by the scale above. The scales are arranged spirally around the center of the cone. Cone scales are made of *lignin wood* (an organic substance with cellulose that makes up the woody tissue of dry wood).

Most conifers have two kinds of cones. Small pollen cones, appearing in the spring, are the male cones and produce pollen. The larger seed cones are the female cones and take from one to three years to produce the seeds. The pollen cones release the pollen and it is blown to the seed cones by the wind. Each pollen grain forms sperm nuclei. In the ovule, the sperm nuclei join with the egg cells that develop in the two ovules on the female cone scales. This produces two seeds on each female cone scale.

Gymnosperms have no ovaries and so their seeds are not enclosed during development. They are covered only by the seed coat. After the seeds mature, the cone opens and the seeds fall out. Many of the seeds have thin, papery, wing-like structures. The wind can carry such seeds a long way.

## Angiosperms

Flowers are the reproductive parts of an angiosperm plant. All flowers have the same basic function—to produce seeds and so preserve the species. The colors, shapes, and fragrance of flowers help the plant to reproduce itself.

Almost all flowers follow the same basic pattern. The average flower is on the tip of a stalk called a *peduncle*. The top of the peduncle is swollen to form a *receptacle*. Above the receptacle, the parts of the flower grow in circles. First come the *sepals*, which are usually green, then the brightly colored *petals*. Inside the petals are the male parts of the flower, the *stamens*. The center of the flower holds the female part, the *pistil*. Only the stamens and pistil are essential to the plant's reproduction.

The sepals are the outermost part of a flower. They are the leaf-like structures on the underside of the flower. Sepals are usually green and cover the unopened bud; later they support the flower after it opens. All the sepals together are called the *calyx*.

The flower petals are the showy, brightly colored part of the flower. They are often colorful to attract bees, butterflies, and other insects for pollination. All the petals together are called the *corolla*.

In order to make seeds, the flowers need male (stamen) and female (pistil) parts. The pistil is the female, seed-bearing part in the center of the flower. It includes the ovary—an enlarged hollow structure at the base of a flower—and a sticky stigma usually found at the tip of a slender style. Inside the ovary are ovules that later become seeds, and eventually fruit.

51 © 2005 AIMS Education Foundation

The pistil is surrounded by the male reproductive parts called stamens. There are two parts to the stamen—the filament and the anther. The anther is the knoblike top of the filament that produces many grains of pollen. Each grain of pollen develops sperm nuclei.

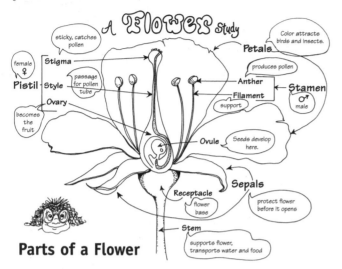

**Parts of a Flower**

Before seeds can develop in the ovary, they must be fertilized by pollen from stamens. Among most flowers, the pollen is carried from the stamens of one flower to the pistil of another flower by wind, insects, or birds. A few flowers self-pollinate.

When a pollen grain lands on the sticky surface of the stigma, the pollen grain swells as it absorbs water, sugar, and other materials from the stigma. The pollen grain then grows a tube through the style until it reaches an ovule in the ovary. Within the ovule, the pollen sperm nuclei fertilizes the egg nucleus. This fertilized egg develops into a seed. The ovary then grows into a structure called the fruit. The fruit encloses and protects the ripening seeds.

Most flowers have four main parts: the sepals, petals, stamens, and pistils. If a flower has all four parts, it is considered complete. If the flower lacks any of the four main parts, it is incomplete. If it has stamens and pistils, the flower is perfect; if it lacks one or the other, it is imperfect.

# Cones and Needles

**Topic**
Conifers (gymnosperms)

**Key Question**
What is a conifer and how does it produce seeds?

**Learning Goal**
Students will examine a conifer plant, cone, and leaves (needles).

**Guiding Documents**
*Project 2061 Benchmark*
- *Scientific investigations may take many different forms, including observing what things are like or what is happening somewhere, collecting specimens for analysis, and doing experiments. Investigations can focus on physical, biological, and social questions.*

*NRC Standards*
- *Scientists use different kinds of investigations depending on the questions they are trying to answer. Types of investigations include describing objects, events, and organisms; classifying them; and doing a fair test (experimenting).*
- *Employ simple equipment and tools to gather data and extend the senses.*

*NCTM Standard 2000\**
- *Select and apply appropriate standard units and tools to measure length, area, volume, weight, time, temperature, and the size of angles*

**Science**
Life science
   botany

**Integrated Processes**
Observing
Collecting and recording data
Comparing and contrasting

**Materials**
*For each group:*
   1 pine cone
   1 pine twig with needles
   centimeter tape
   balance
   gram masses

**mature cone**
**(open)**

**Background Information**
Trees that produce cones as a protective covering for their seeds are called conifers. The term conifer means cone-bearing tree. Most conifers have leaves that are sharp and slender like a needle. With few exceptions, they are evergreen and do not lose their leaves in the winter. The conifers belong to a large division of the plant world, the gymnosperms.

The term gymnosperm means that there is no ovary or fruit surrounding the embryo and endosperm of the seed. Instead, each seed develops between the scales of the female cone. Most conifers also have male cones in which pollen is produced. An immature cone is green and closed. As the cones mature, they dry and open, allowing the seeds to escape and fly on the wind.

One of the most plentiful groups of trees, conifers include pine, spruce, fir, hemlock, redwood, and cedar. These form extensive forests and provide an important source of lumber, wood pulp, pine tar, resins, and turpentine.

Conifers are some of the largest and longest-living plants on Earth. The bristle cone pines, found in the mountains of California, are about 4600 years old. The redwood trees can be 90 meters tall; the General Sherman Tree in Sequoia National Park is 2000 years old, measures 11 meters in diameter, and weighs 5594 metric tons.

The other great division of seed-bearing plants are the angiosperms; the seeds are enclosed in fruits. These include most of our fruit, nut, and vegetable plants.

**Management**
1. Obtain some cones and conifer branches. (Pine is the most abundant conifer. There are several different kinds of pines in any area so try to get different types of cones. If possible, get some cones that are mature and some that are immature and still have the seeds in the cones.)
2. Collect twigs of conifers with leaves (needles).
3. Have students work in cooperative groups of four.
4. You can open the scales of a seed cone by boiling an immature pine cone in water. The students can then see the two seeds that lie on top of each scale. You may also be able to find seeds between the bottom scales of older pine cones, the top scales of which have already opened.
5. If you are unable to find any seeds in the cones, you can buy pine nuts (seeds) in many stores that sell nuts.

 © 2005 AIMS Education Foundation

## Procedure

1. Ask students to brainstorm places where they have seen cones. [in a forest, in stores, on Christmas trees] What are the cones for? Explain that cones are the part of the plant that contains seeds.

2. Tell students that plants that produce cones are called conifers, a term that means cone-bearing. Inform them that conifers belong to a group of woody plants called gymnosperms that produce seeds with no outer covering. The gymnosperm seed is found between the scales of a cone. The seed has no ovary or fruit surrounding the embryo and endosperm. Most of the gymnosperms with which they will become familiar are conifers. Point out that sequoias, red-woods, and bristle cone pines are conifers that all hold some kind of longevity or size records.

cross section of cone with seeds

3. Give each group a pine cone to observe. Have them describe the color, shape, smell, and feel to each other and record on the activity sheet.

4. Instruct each group to count the number of scales, measure the length and circumference (around the largest part of the cone), and find the mass.

5. Have groups remove one cone scale, then observe and draw it. There should be a pair of winged seeds at the base. It is possible the seeds are missing, but the slight depressions in which the seeds rested can be seen.

scale with 2 seeds

6. Direct students to look at the base of the cone and observe the spiral pattern of the cone scales. Follow the line of these to the top.

7. Guide the groups as they share their observations with the class, then exchange and compare cones.

8. Give each group a pine twig. Instruct them to carefully examine and describe how it looks, smells, and feels. (Have them include whether the needles are singly attached or in bundles of two, three, or five.)

9. Have students measure branch length and needle length and draw the branch.

## Connecting Learning

1. How would you describe a conifer?
2. How is a pine tree leaf different from that of a broadleaf tree? [A pine leaf (needle) is long and narrow while a broadleaf is large and flat.]
3. Describe a cone from a conifer.
4. Where are the seeds in a cone? [between the scales of the female cone]
5. What are you wondering now?

## Extensions

1. Discuss the importance of conifer products: lumber, paper, and other forestry products. Discuss the role of conifers (food, protection, shelter) in forests as part of the community and food web.

2. Divide the class into small groups. Assign each group a specific conifer to study. Have them gather information about their conifer's appearance, importance, distribution, and uses. Encourage them to include pictures, drawings, or specimens.

3. Let students take the pine seeds from the cones or, if not available, give them pine nuts. Have them observe the seeds and remove the hard seed coat. They should be able to split the seed with their fingernails so they can observe the plant embryo.

seed

## Curriculum Correlations

*Art*

Use the cones as subjects for pencil and charcoal sketches. Have students draw the cones much larger than life on 12"x 18" paper, adding shading and shadows. Display on a bulletin board.

*Social Studies*

1. Research the history and economic importance of the Douglas fir tree.
2. Take a trip to a lumber yard to find out what kinds of wood they sell.

*Music*

Sing *Trail of the Lonesome Pine*, a traditional cowboy song.

\* Reprinted with permission from *Principles and Standards for School Mathematics,* 2000 by the National Council of Teachers of Mathematics. All rights reserved.

# Cones and Needles

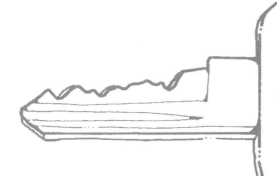

## Key Question

What is a conifer and how does it produce seeds?

## Learning Goal

Students will:

- examine a conifer plant, cone, and leaves (needles).

 © 2005 AIMS Education Foundation

# Cones and Needles

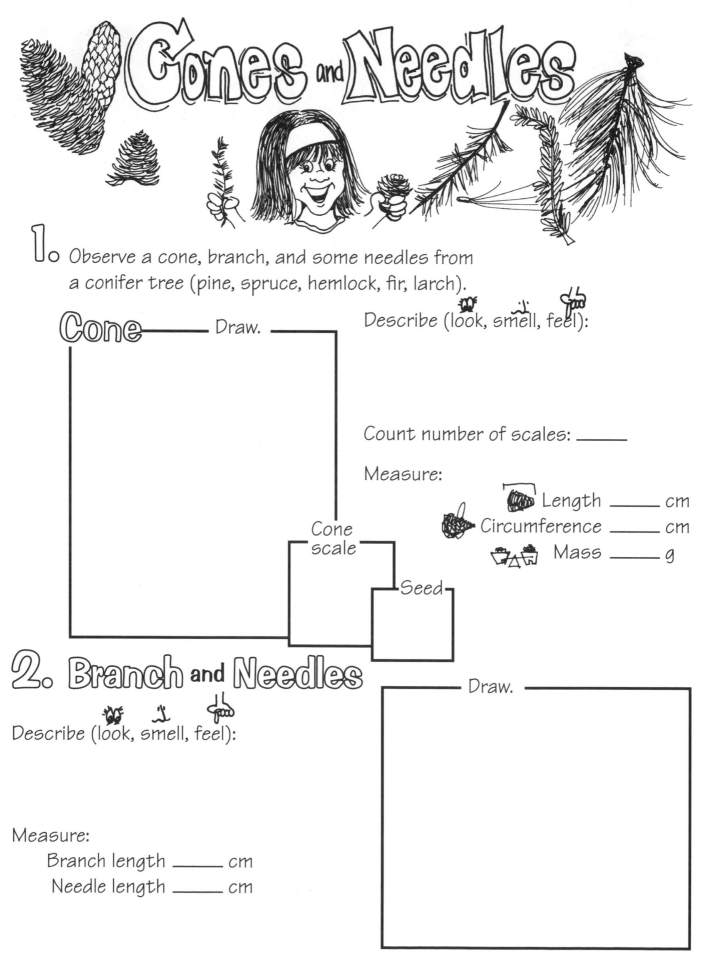

1. Observe a cone, branch, and some needles from a conifer tree (pine, spruce, hemlock, fir, larch).

## Cone ——— Draw. ———

Describe (look, smell, feel):

Count number of scales: _____

Measure:

Length _____ cm
Circumference _____ cm
Mass _____ g

Cone scale

Seed

## 2. Branch and Needles

Describe (look, smell, feel):

Draw.

Measure:
Branch length _____ cm
Needle length _____ cm

# Cones and Needles

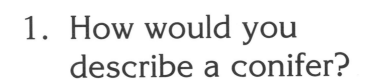

1. How would you describe a conifer?

2. How is a pine tree leaf different from that of a broadleaf tree?

3. Describe a cone from a conifer.

4. Where are the seeds in a cone?

5. What are you wondering now?

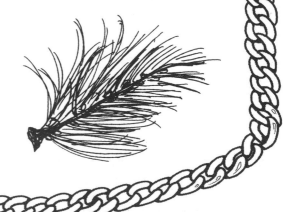

                    © 2005 AIMS Education Foundation

# History of a Tree

## Topic
Age of a tree

## Key Question
How can we determine the age of a tree?

## Learning Goal
Students will observe a tree's rings to approximate its age.

## Guiding Documents
*Project 2061 Benchmark*
- *Scientific investigations may take many different forms, including observing what things are like or what is happening somewhere, collecting specimens for analysis, and doing experiments. Investigations can focus on physical, biological, and social questions.*

*NRC Standards*
- *Employ simple equipment and tools to gather data and extend the senses.*
- *Simple instruments, such as magnifiers, thermometers, and rulers, provide more information than scientists obtain using only their senses.*
- *Each plant or animal has different structures that serve different functions in growth, survival, and reproduction. For example, humans have distinct body structures for walking, holding, seeing, and talking.*

## Science
Life science
  botany
    trees

## Integrated Processes
Observing
Comparing and contrasting
Collecting and recording data
Generalizing

## Materials
*For the class:*
  overhead transparency of *History of a Tree* fact sheet

*For each group:*
  tree rounds (see *Management 1*)
  rulers
  metric tape measure
  hand lens, 1 per person

## Background Information
Trees are the biggest and oldest plants on Earth. They continue to grow as long as they live, which can be for hundreds or thousands of years.

Tree growth depends on water, temperature, and location of the plant. The annual growth rings can show how the weather has changed over the years. Counting the rings of a tree gives a fairly accurate measure of a tree's age. The wider the rings, the more growth of the tree and the closer to ideal the weather conditions have been. Narrow rings indicate less growth due to cold weather or drought conditions.

The bark on the outside of the trunk protects the tree. Beneath that is the cambium layer where new wood grows. The cells of the cambium keep dividing to create new cells on either side of it. These cells line up to become the tree's transportation structures, phloem and xylem. Phloem (inner bark), the tubes on the outer side of the cambium, carry food made by the leaves. Xylem (sapwood), on the inner side on the cambium, transports water and dissolved minerals in sap from the roots to the rest of the tree. As the tree grows, chemical deposits build up inside the older xylem, causing this part of the sapwood to stop functioning as a transport system; it has become heartwood, the dark, hard core that supports the tree.

Each year's growth ring has both light and dark wood. In spring, the cambium grows quickly and the ring is light-colored. The ring is darker at the end of each growing season as the cambium grows more slowly.

## Management
1. Places to obtain tree rounds include the U.S. Forestry Department or a tree trimming business. Sometimes the rounds are from saplings or branches. The round of a tree limb will not tell the age of the tree, only the age of that limb; however, the process of counting tree rings will be the same.
2. Each group should have one or more tree rounds. These can be rotated from group to group.
3. To help explain how the age of a tree is obtained, make a transparency of the *History of a Tree* fact sheet.

## Procedure

1. Discuss with students how a tree grows. Just beneath the bark is the cambium layer. Growth in the cambium adds cells to the layer (which then becomes a yearly ring) and increases the circumference of the tree.
2. Use the overhead transparency of a tree round to explain the tree parts and what students should look for in their rounds.
3. Explain that it is difficult to accurately tell the age of a tree without counting the rings; this usually means the tree has to be cut down. Foresters now have an instrument that can bore a thin tube of the tree so that tree rings can be counted without cutting down the tree.
4. Distribute *How Old was the Tree?*, the tree rounds, and tape measures.
5. Have students make a pencil rubbing of their tree rounds and identify the different parts.
6. Instruct students to measure the diameter and circumference, then count the rings and record the age of the tree when it was cut down.
7. To determine when the tree germinated, have students subtract the number of rings from the present year.

## Connecting Learning

1. In what part of the tree is new wood growing?

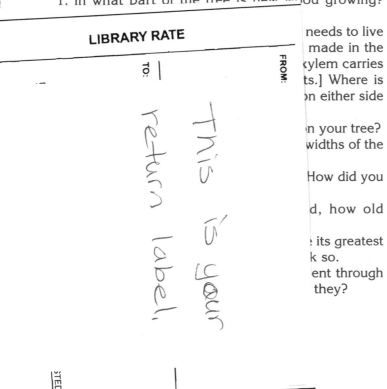

**LIBRARY RATE**

TO:

FROM:

This is your return label.

needs to live
made in the
xylem carries
ts.] Where is
on either side

n your tree?
widths of the

How did you

d, how old

its greatest
k so.
ent through
they?

## Extension

The largest living thing on Earth is the General Sherman Tree, a sequoia tree in California. Its trunk is over 24 meters around. Measure a 24-meter string and tie the ends together to make a circle. Spread the circle out in the cafeteria or outside on the playground. Have the children link hands, stand around the circle, and imagine the immense size of the tree trunk.

## Curriculum Correlations

### Language Arts

Research some of the ancient trees that are still living today, such as bristlecone pine. Make reports on various kinds of trees.

### Social Studies

Imagine a world without trees. Discuss how people and animals would be affected.

### Art

1. Sketch a tree.
2. Do bark rubbings on a tree.
3. Design a poster to save our forests.

# History of a Tree

## Key Question

How can we determine the age of a tree?

## Learning Goal

### Students will:

- observe a tree's rings to approximate its age.

# History of a Tree

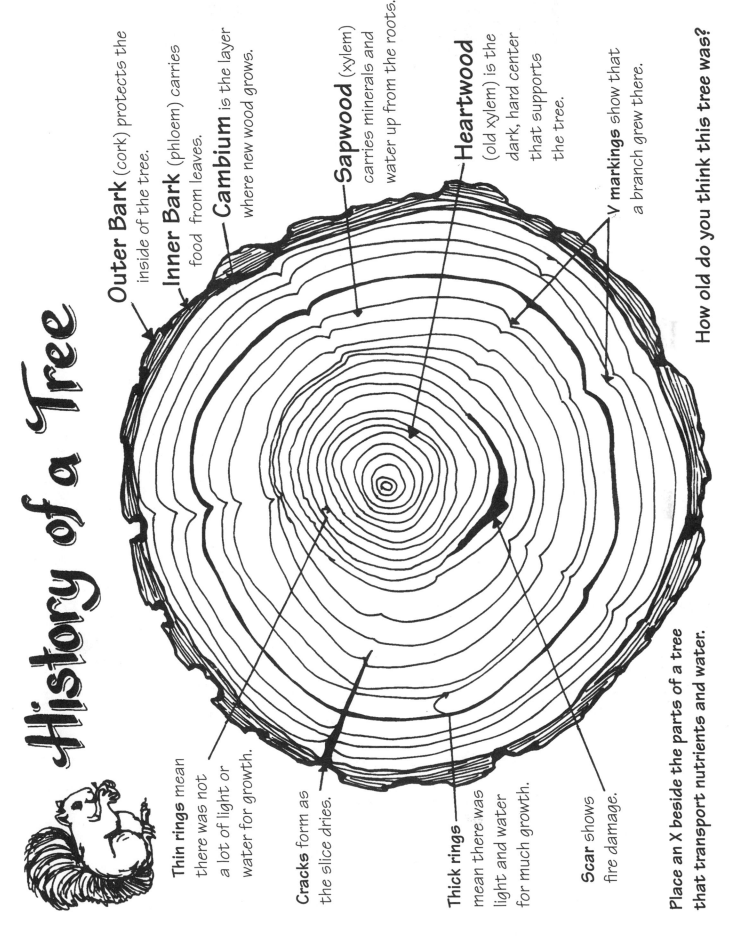

**Outer Bark** (cork) protects the inside of the tree.

**Inner Bark** (phloem) carries food from leaves.

**Cambium** is the layer where new wood grows.

**Sapwood** (xylem) carries minerals and water up from the roots.

**Heartwood** (old xylem) is the dark, hard center that supports the tree.

**V markings** show that a branch grew there.

**Thin rings** mean there was not a lot of light or water for growth.

**Cracks** form as the slice dries.

**Thick rings** mean there was light and water for much growth.

**Scar** shows fire damage.

How old do you think this tree was?

Place an X beside the parts of a tree that transport nutrients and water.

# History of a Tree

## How old was the tree?

Make a pencil rubbing
of your tree slice.

### Measure

Diameter: _____ cm

Circumference: _____ cm

### Count

Number of rings: _____

Age of the tree: _____

What year did this tree germinate (begin to grow)? _____

 © 2005 AIMS Education Foundation

# History of a Tree

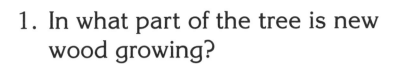

1.  In what part of the tree is new wood growing?

2.  How does the tree get the nutrients it needs to live and grow? Where is this transportation system located?

3.  What did you notice about the rings on your tree?

4.  What would account for the different widths of the rings?

5.  What year did the tree start to grow? How did you figure this out?

6.  When your tree was five years old, how old were you?

7.  What time of the year does a tree have its greatest growth? Explain why you think so.

8.  Were there any signs that your tree went through some hard times in its life? What were they?

9.  What are you wondering now?

 © 2005 AIMS Education Foundation

# Observe a Tree

## Topic
Observe a tree

## Key Question
How would you describe a tree?

## Learning Goals
Students will:
- observe a tree's features, and
- estimate the tree's height.

## Guiding Documents
*Project 2061 Benchmark*
- *Scientific investigations may take many different forms, including observing what things are like or what is happening somewhere, collecting specimens for analysis, and doing experiments. Investigations can focus on physical, biological, and social questions.*

*NRC Standards*
- *Scientists use different kinds of investigations depending on the questions they are trying to answer. Types of investigations include describing objects, events, and organisms; classifying them; and doing a fair test (experimenting).*
- *Employ simple equipment and tools to gather data and extend the senses.*

*NCTM Standard 2000\**
- *Select and apply appropriate standard units and tools to measure length, area, volume, weight, time, temperature, and the size of angles*

## Science
Life science
  botany

## Integrated Processes
Observing
Collecting and recording data

## Materials
*For each student:*
  a tree on the school ground
  centimeter tape

## Background Information
Trees are useful to us in many ways. The fruit of trees is used for food. The wood can be used for lumber, furniture, building materials, and for fuel. Trees are also important to humans for beauty, shade, and enjoyment. Trees are also home to many birds, insects, and animals.

Through this activity, the students will become more aware of trees and the changes that occur through the year. They should also begin to realize that there are many different kinds of trees.

## Management
Beforehand, if possible, identify the trees on the playground by type.

## Procedure
1. Brainstorm with students all the ways that we use trees. Have them record their answers on the *How do we use trees?* sheet.
2. Take students outside to find all the trees that are growing on the playground. If you can, identify the trees by name for the students.
3. Suggest each student pick one tree to observe, first from a distance and then up close. Distribute the second sheet and have them record their observations.
4. Instruct students to write a descriptive paragraph using the picture words they have chosen.
5. Give students *Measure a Tree* and centimeter tapes. Have them measure in hand spans, footsteps, and metric units. Encourage them to measure tree height using the method explained on the sheet. They can also use a proportion comparing the shadow lengths of a meter stick and a tree to determine height.

$$\frac{\text{length of meter stick shadow}}{100 \text{ cm (height of meter stick)}} = \frac{\text{length of tree shadow}}{x \text{ (height of tree)}}$$

6. Distribute *Tree Portrait*. Advise students to pick up natural material around their trees (fallen twigs, leaves, bark, seeds, etc.) and use these to make pictures of their trees.

## Connecting Learning

1. Why did you choose the tree that you did?
2. What different living things did you see in the tree? [insects, birds, squirrel, etc.]
3. Trees in the same family have similar characteristics. Who chose a tree that might belong in the same family as your tree? Why do you think so?
4. What are some ways people use trees?
5. What are you wondering now?

## Extensions

1. Find an especially large tree in the neighborhood. Measure its height and circumference.
2. Discuss the changes made by the tree throughout the year.

## Curriculum Correlation

*Language Arts*

Write a cinquain poem about a tree (one noun, two adjectives, three verbs, four or five words expressing a feeling, synonym for the first word).

> tree
> tall, green
> spreading, sheltering, swaying
> cooling relief from the heat
> leafy tower

*Social Studies*

Research famous trees noted for their height, size, age, etc.

* Reprinted with permission from *Principles and Standards for School Mathematics,* 2000 by the National Council of Teachers of Mathematics. All rights reserved.

# Observe a Tree

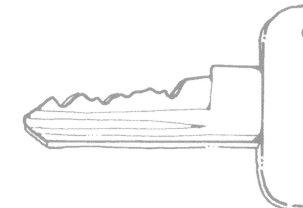

## Key Question

How would you describe a tree?

## Learning Goals

### Students will:

- observe a tree's features, and

- estimate the tree's height.

# Observe a Tree

## How do we use trees?

We use trees for:

1. _____
2. _____
3. _____
4. _____
5. _____
6. _____
7. _____
8. _____
9. _____

10. _____
11. _____
12. _____
13. _____
14. _____
15. _____
16. _____
17. _____
18. _____
19. _____
20. _____
21. _____
22. _____
23. _____

24. _____
25. _____
26. _____
27. _____
28. _____
29. _____
30. _____
31. _____
32. _____
33. _____
34. _____
35. _____
36. _____
37. _____

If you can think of any more, write them on the back!

© 2005 AIMS Education Foundation

# Observe a Tree

1. View the tree from a distance. Describe its general shape and size.

 2. Move closer to the tree. Touch the tree. Describe the texture of its bark, leaves, and branches.

 3. What are the colors in your tree?

 4. What unique features does your tree display? (scars, etc.)

 5. Write a paragraph that uses at least five picture words that will help others "see" your tree.

1. _____

2. _____

3. _____

4. _____

5. _____

My tree is a friend.

# Observe a Tree

## Measure a Tree

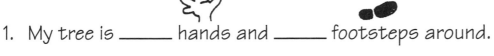

1. My tree is _____ hands and _____ footsteps around.

2. My tree is _____ centimeters around.

3. My tree's shadow is _____ meters long.

4. I think my tree is _____ meters tall.

Measure the height of your tree.

Measure the height of the tree this way:
Hold on to your ankles and walk away from the tree until you can see the top of the tree through your legs. Turn around and measure the number of meters back to the tree.

5. My tree is about _____ meters tall.

# Observe a Tree
## Tree Portrait

Use natural materials to make a picture of your tree.

Artist:

 © 2005 AIMS Education Foundation

# Observe a Tree

1. Why did you choose the tree that you did?

2. What different living things did you see in the tree?

3. Trees in the same family have similar characteristics. Who chose a tree that might belong in the same family as your tree? Why do you think so?

4. What are some ways people use trees?

5. What are you wondering now?

# A Flower Study

## Topic
Parts of a flower and seed development

## Key Question
How do flowers, seeds, and fruit develop in a plant?

## Learning Goal
Students will identify parts of a flower and their function in developing seeds.

## Guiding Documents
*Project 2061 Benchmark*
- *Scientific investigations may take many different forms, including observing what things are like or what is happening somewhere, collecting specimens for analysis, and doing experiments. Investigations can focus on physical, biological, and social questions.*

*NRC Standard*
- *Each plant or animal has different structures that serve different functions in growth, survival, and reproduction. For example, humans have distinct body structures for walking, holding, seeing, and talking.*

*NCTM Standard 2000\**
- *Select and apply appropriate standard units and tools to measure length, area, volume, weight, time, temperature, and the size of angles*

## Math
Measurement
  length

## Science
Life science
  botany

## Integrated Processes
Observing
Collecting and recording data
Comparing and contrasting

## Materials
*For each group:*
  1 flower (see *Management 1*)
  hand lens (or field microscope)
  small square of black paper
  metric ruler

*For the class:*
  overhead transparency of *Parts of a Flower*
  1 or more pea pods

## Background Information
The flower is the reproductive part of a plant. Most flowers have four main parts: the sepals, petals, stamens, and pistils. If a flower has all four parts, it is complete. If it does not have these four parts, it is considered to be an incomplete flower. All flowers have the same basic function—to produce seeds and so preserve the species. The colors, shapes, and fragrance of flowers help the plant to reproduce itself.

Botanists define fruit as the ripened ovary and seed of a flowering plant. Fruits have many different structures. Some are fleshy, like peaches, grapes, squash, and tomatoes. Others are hard and dry, like sunflower seeds, corn, and wheat. Others have nothing to do with food, like the prickly burs on a puncture vine or the wispy parachutes of dandelions. The function of fruit is to protect the seeds and to assist with dispersal.

## Management
1. Obtain complete flowers, preferably of the same variety. It is easiest to see the ovary and seeds in tulips, daffodils, gladioli, lilies, and gloxinia.
2. After students have dissected a flower and are acquainted with its parts, have them bring in other varieties of flowers for comparison.
3. The pistil needs to be split lengthwise. Perhaps an adult will need to do the cutting.

## Procedure

1. Ask students to brainstorm the names of all the flowers they know. Record the names on chart paper, a transparency, or the board.
2. Discuss why plants have flowers. [reproduction] Talk about all the colors of flowers and why colors are necessary to flowers. [pollination by birds and insects]
3. Use the *Parts of a Flower* transparency to introduce the name, location, and function of each part.

    Sepals: leaflike parts at the base of the flower, usually green, that protect it before it opens

    Petals: brightly colored to attract insects or birds

    Stamen: makes pollen (male part)

    Pistil: produces seeds (female part)

    Receptacle: base where the flower is attached, supports the flower

    Stem: supports the flower and transports water and food

4. Give each group a flower and hand lens and each student the first observation sheet. Have them carefully study the flower, record their observations, and write a detailed description.
5. Distribute the second observation sheet. Have students remove the sepals, then sketch, count, and measure them.
6. Direct students to remove the petals and record their observations.
7. Have students detach the stamens, identify the anther (top part) and filament (stalk-like part), and record their observations.
8. Explain that the anther contains the grains of pollen or male cells needed to fertilize flowers. Pollen is carried from flower to flower by bees, wasps, birds, wind, etc. To make a pollen print, press the anthers against a piece of black paper.
9. Review the three parts of the pistil—the stigma, style, and ovary. Seeds are produced in the ovary.
10. Have students remove the pistil and record their observations. Tell them the stigma is the sticky upper end to which pollen grains cling. After the stigma receives the pollen, the pollen grains grow tubes down through the narrow style into the ovary. The ovary has ovules containing the egg cells. Fertilization occurs when a male pollen grain and a female egg cell unite. A seed begins to develop and grow.
11. Split the pistil lengthwise and instruct students to look for the ovules inside the ovary. Inform them that, after fertilization, the ovary ripens into a fruit that helps protect the seeds that develop from the ovules. Open a pea pod; the pod is the ovary and the peas are the mature ovules.
12. Have students use the back of the paper to explain the function of each part of the flower.

## Connecting Learning

1. What is the purpose of a flower? [to produce seeds]
2. In what part of the flower do seeds develop? [ovary]
3. What is the male part of the flower? [stamen] How does it help with reproduction? [produces pollen]
4. Name some ways pollen is scattered to other flowers. [bees, wind, wasps]
5. How do petals help? [The color attracts insects and birds that might brush against the pollen and carry it to another flower.]
6. What is the female part of the flower? [pistil] How does it help with reproduction? [Pollen clings to the sticky stigma. It travels down the style to the ovary where it joins with the ovule to produce a seed.]
7. Why is it an advantage for the stigma to be sticky? [Pollen will cling better.]
8. If you took a flower apart, what four parts might you find? [sepals, petals, stamens, and pistils]
9. What are you wondering now?

## Extensions

1. Cut an apple and have students observe. Explain that the seeds are in the ovary and the receptacle, or base of the flower, is the fleshy part we eat.
2. Cut open and have students compare the undeveloped ovary of a rose with the mature ovary of a rose hip, the fruit of the rose.
3. Encourage students to collect other flowering plants and identify the major parts.
4. Plant seeds of flowering plants and observe how the plants grow.
5. Discuss and list everyday uses for flowers.

## Curriculum Correlation

*Art*

Press some flowers. When they are dry, glue them to a piece of tagboard and cover with clear cellophane wrap. They can also be enclosed in two sheets of clear contact paper. Hang in a window.

\*   Reprinted with permission from *Principles and Standards for School Mathematics,* 2000 by the National Council of Teachers of Mathematics. All rights reserved.

# A Flower Study

## Key Question

How do flowers, seeds, and fruit develop in a plant?

## Learning Goal

**Students will:**

- identify parts of a flower and their function in developing seeds.

# A Flower Study

## Parts of a Flower

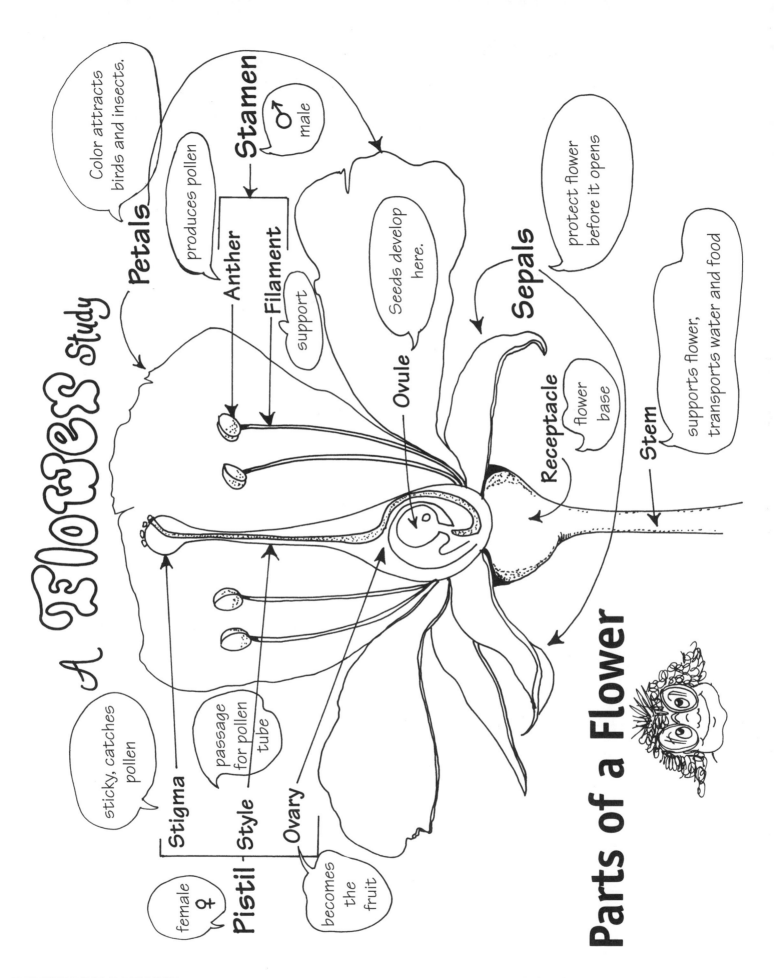

Petals — Color attracts birds and insects.

Stamen ♂ male

Anther — produces pollen

Filament — support

Ovule — Seeds develop here.

Sepals — protect flower before it opens

Receptacle — flower base

Stem — supports flower, transports water and food

Stigma — sticky, catches pollen

Style — passage for pollen tube

Ovary — becomes the fruit

Pistil ♀ female

# A Flower Study

1. Get a close-up look at a flower. Study the flower from all angles with a hand lens.

   Observations:

2. Use pencil and colors to sketch your flower.

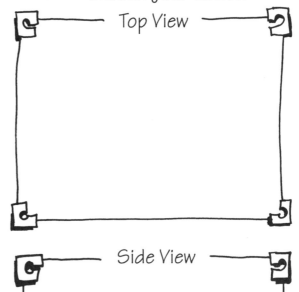

Top View

Side View

3. Use your notes to write a description of your flower so that anyone could pick it out from a bunch.

# A Flower Study

Carefully remove each flower part.
Sketch, count, and measure.

| Flower Part | | Sketch | Number (count) | Color | Length (average) |
|---|---|---|---|---|---|
| Sepals | | | | | |
| Petals | | | | | |
| Stamen | anther | | | | |
| | filament | | | | |
| Pistil | stigma | | | | |
| | style | | | | |
| | ovary | | | | |
| Receptacle | | | | | |
| Stem | | | | | |

What is the function of each part of the flower?

© 2005 AIMS Education Foundation

# A Flower Study

CONNECTING LEARNING

1.  What is the purpose of a flower?

2.  In what part of the flower do seeds develop?

3.  What is the male part of the flower? How does it help with reproduction?

4.  Name some ways pollen is scattered to other flowers.

5.  How do petals help?

6.  What is the female part of the flower? How does it help with reproduction?

7.  Why is it an advantage for the stigma to be sticky?

8.  If you took a flower apart, what four parts might you find?

9.  What are you wondering now?

# Seeds from FRUITS

**Topic**
Comparing fruit and vegetable seeds

**Key Question**
Where are seeds found in the fruit of flowering plants?

**Learning Goal**
Students will compare seeds that are produced in several flowering plants.

**Guiding Documents**
*Project 2061 Benchmark*
- *Scientific investigations may take many different forms, including observing what things are like or what is happening somewhere, collecting specimens for analysis, and doing experiments. Investigations can focus on physical, biological, and social questions.*

*NRC Standards*
- *Scientists use different kinds of investigations depending on the questions they are trying to answer. Types of investigations include describing objects, events, and organisms; classifying them; and doing a fair test (experimenting).*
- *Employ simple equipment and tools to gather data and extend the senses.*

*NCTM Standard 2000\**
- *Select and apply appropriate standard units and tools to measure length, area, volume, weight, time, temperature, and the size of angles*

**Math**
Measurement
    mass
Whole number operations
    percent
Graphing
    bar

**Science**
Life science
    botany
        seeds

**Integrated Processes**
Observing
Collecting and recording data
Comparing and contrasting
Relating

**Materials**
*For each group:*
    1 or more fruits with seeds (see *Management 1*)
    paper towels and paper plates
    balance
    gram masses
    calculators, optional

*For the class:*
    1 or more sharp knives (see *Management 3*)

**Background Information**
Some seeds are enclosed and protected; others are naked or uncovered. Angiosperms produce enclosed, protected seeds.

After the egg cells of a flower are fertilized, seeds begin to develop. The ovary ripens into the fruit, providing a protective structure around the seeds. The fruit can be juicy like a peach or apple, or dry like a peanut or bean. The sweet, juicy, and brightly-colored fruits are readily eaten by animals, so the seeds are scattered far from the parent plant.

Not all fruit are formed in the same way. In the peach, the sweet, fleshy part we eat is the ovary of the plant. In the apple, it is the receptacle of the flower and the floral tube; the ovary is the apple core. In the orange, we eat the fleshy tissue of the ovary; the seeds are embedded in the flesh. In the pea and bean pods, the pod is the ovary wall; the peas and beans are the seeds of the plant.

Botanically, the term vegetable is a generic word that we use to indicate the edible parts of plants that include stem, leaves, bulbs, roots, flowers, and fruits. In this activity, the term fruit is used to indicate any fruit or vegetable that has an edible, protective flesh around the seeds. A fruit always develops from a flower and is always composed of at least one ripened and matured ovary.

**:ment**

.ɪoose fruits such as apples, Valencia oranges, peaches, pea pods, cucumbers, grapes, tomatoes, bell peppers, etc.

2. Divide the class into groups of three or four. Each group should have at least one fruit. They will report their data for the rest of the class to record, as needed.

3. If you feel it is safe to do so, have students cut the fruit. Otherwise, have an adult do the cutting. Do not cut beforehand.

4. It is advisable for students to wash their hands before handling the fruit.

## Procedure

1. Explain that seeds are protected by the fruit that surrounds them. Apples, tomatoes, cucumbers, peaches, citrus, peas, grapes, beans, and nuts (and many other fruits) all have protected seeds.

2. Distribute the observation sheet and one or more fruits to each group. Tell them that groups will share data so that they can complete all six labels.

3. Instruct students to measure the mass of each fruit before it is cut.

4. Using a sharp knife and paper towels, cut or have students cut the fruit in half lengthwise. Ask them to draw a cross section of the fruits showing where the seeds are located.

5. For each fruit, have students count the number of seeds and measure their mass.

6. Guide groups as they share their data for the rest of the class to record.

7. Give students the bar graph. Ask them what data they want to graph—the number of seeds or the mass of the fruit. Have them list the fruits, number and label the top part of the graph, and color it.

8. If appropriate for your class, distribute the sheet on percents. Model how to figure the percentage of seed mass to fruit mass (seed mass ÷ fruit mass). Have students calculate the percentages, rounded if desired, and complete the graph.

For the orange data shown—

Divide:     $3 \div 211$    $= .014$

Multiply:  $.014 \times 100 = 1.4\%$

9. Assist groups in sharing and discussing their results.

## Connecting Learning

1. Where are the seeds formed?
2. How are the seeds of each fruit protected? [by fleshy fruit with skin or rind (grapes, oranges, and many others), by pods (peas, beans), by shells (nuts)]
3. How does the number of seeds from each fruit compare? Which fruits have only one seed?
4. Are the size of the seed and the size of the fruit related? Explain.
5. Which seeds do we normally eat?
6. What are you wondering now?

## Extensions

1. Use the fruit to make a salad for students to enjoy.
2. Save the seeds. A few days later, have students identify which seeds go with which fruit.

## Curriculum Correlation

*Social Studies*

Have students research the origins of their favorite fruit.

\* Reprinted with permission from *Principles and Standards for School Mathematics,* 2000 by the National Council of Teachers of Mathematics. All rights reserved.

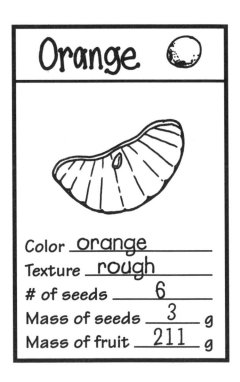

Orange

Color __orange__
Texture __rough__
# of seeds ____6____
Mass of seeds ___3___ g
Mass of fruit __211__ g

# Seeds from FRUITS

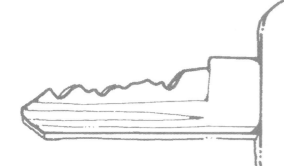

## Key Question

Where are seeds found in the fruit of flowering plants?

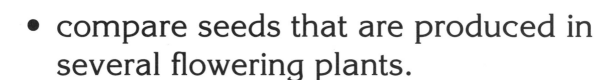

## Learning Goal

### Students will:

- compare seeds that are produced in several flowering plants.

Draw and color a section of each fruit. Record all data.

| Apple |
|---|
| |
| Color _____ |
| Texture _____ |
| # of seeds _____ |
| Mass of seeds _____ g |
| Mass of fruit _____ g |

| |
|---|
| |
| Color _____ |
| Texture _____ |
| # of seeds _____ |
| Mass of seeds _____ g |
| Mass of fruit _____ g |

| |
|---|
| |
| Color _____ |
| Texture _____ |
| # of seeds _____ |
| Mass of seeds _____ g |
| Mass of fruit _____ g |

| |
|---|
| |
| Color _____ |
| Texture _____ |
| # of seeds _____ |
| Mass of seeds _____ g |
| Mass of fruit _____ g |

| |
|---|
| |
| Color _____ |
| Texture _____ |
| # of seeds _____ |
| Mass of seeds _____ g |
| Mass of fruit _____ g |

| |
|---|
| |
| Color _____ |
| Texture _____ |
| # of seeds _____ |
| Mass of seeds _____ g |
| Mass of fruit _____ g |

# Seeds from FRUITS

Choose the data you want to show on the bar graph.
Label and complete the graph.

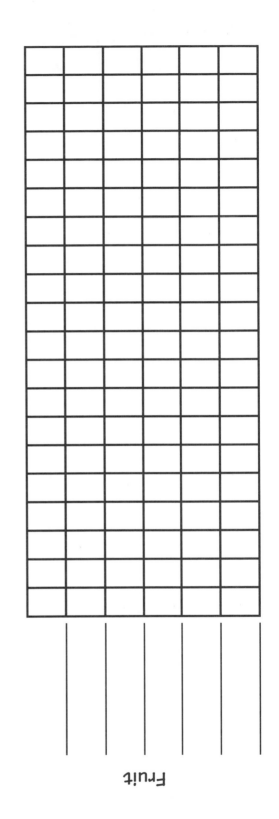

Fruit

# Seeds from FRUITS

## What percent of the total mass of each fruit are the seeds?

To figure the percent, divide seed mass by fruit mass and multiply by 100. Record below and complete the bar graph.

| Fruit | % |
|-------|---|
|       |   |

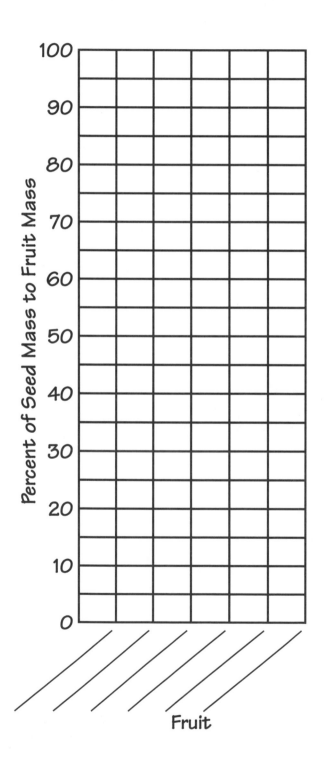

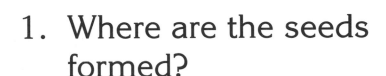

1. Where are the seeds formed?

2. How are the seeds of each fruit protected?

3. How do the number of seeds from each fruit compare? Which fruits have only one seed?

4. Are the size of the seed and the size of the fruit related? Explain.

5. Which seeds do we normally eat?

6. What are you wondering now?

# Plant Structure Facts

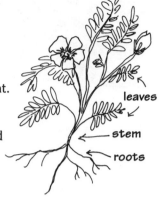

## Roots

Roots serve several purposes. They anchor the plant to the ground. Numerous fine root hairs absorb water and minerals from the soil needed for plant growth. In some plants, roots store food for plant use.

There are two main types of root systems—fibrous and taproot. The fibrous root system is a mass of branching roots spreading in all directions from the base of the stem. More of a plant's mass is often below ground than above ground. Most monocots, such as grasses, have a fibrous root system; so do weeds.

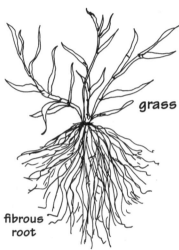

grass

fibrous root

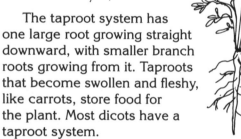

poppy

taproot

The taproot system has one large root growing straight downward, with smaller branch roots growing from it. Taproots that become swollen and fleshy, like carrots, store food for the plant. Most dicots have a taproot system.

People use roots as a source of food. Carrots, beets, sweet potatoes, radishes, turnips, rutabagas, parsnips, and cassava (tapioca) are all root foods. Spices such as sassafras, sarsaparilla, and licorice are obtained from roots. Other root products include drugs, insecticides, dyes, and poisons.

## Stems and Twigs

The stem supports the leaves and flowers of a plant. It also transports the water and minerals to the rest of the plant. Water is absorbed by the roots and moves up through the narrow xylem tubes in the stem to the leaves and flowers.

leaves

stem

roots

Transpiration is the evaporation of water from the stomata—tiny openings on the surface of the leaves. The loss of water through the stomata helps pull up more water from the roots.

Almost all plants have stems. They can vary in size from the extremely short stem of a lettuce plant to the towering trunk of a redwood tree.

Stems that people eat include celery, asparagus, bamboo shoots, and rhubarb. White potatoes are swollen underground stems called tubers. Sugar is extracted from sugar cane stems. Maple sugar comes from the sap in maple tree trunks.

A tree adds new growth at the tip of each branch and twig. Trees can be identified during dormancy by the shape and the arrangement—opposite, alternate, or clustered—of the buds and accompanying leaf scars on the twigs and also by the bundle scars.

The terminal bud at the tip of a stem is protected by bud scales during winter dormancy. When the bud begins its spring growth, these scales are shed, leaving bud scale scars that circle the stem. The terminal bud adds height to a tree.

Lateral buds grow on the sides of the stem. They contain shoots that develop into lateral leaf-bearing twigs.

The places on the stem where leaves are attached and lateral buds develop are called nodes. The space between two nodes is an internode. The length of the internode depends on growing conditions.

The leaf scar, where the leaf was attached to the twig, has small, raised dots called bundle scars. The dots are the ends of the xylem tubes.

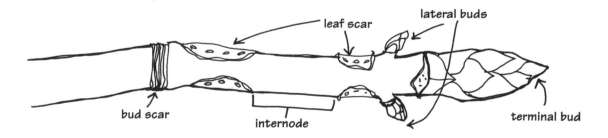

leaf scar

lateral buds

bud scar

internode

terminal bud

## Topic
Roots

## Key Question
What does a plant's root system look like?

## Learning Goal
Students will observe the root system of a plant and compare it with the growth above ground.

## Guiding Documents
*Project 2061 Benchmark*
- *Scientific investigations may take many different forms, including observing what things are like or what is happening somewhere, collecting specimens for analysis, and doing experiments. Investigations can focus on physical, biological, and social questions.*

*NRC Standards*
- *Employ simple equipment and tools to gather data and extend the senses.*
- *Simple instruments, such as magnifiers, thermometers, and rulers, provide more information than scientists obtain using only their senses.*
- *Each plant or animal has different structures that serve different functions in growth, survival, and reproduction. For example, humans have distinct body structures for walking, holding, seeing, and talking.*

*NCTM Standard 2000\**
- *Select and apply appropriate standard units and tools to measure length, area, volume, weight, time, temperature, and the size of angles*

## Math
Measurement
    length

## Science
Life science
    botany
        roots

## Integrated Processes
Observing
Comparing and contrasting
Collecting and recording data
Generalizing

## Materials
*For each group:*
    plant with fibrous roots (see *Management 2*)
    digging tool
    metric ruler
    newspaper
    paper towel
    reclosable plastic bag
    strip of two-sided tape
    4 radish seeds
    hand lens

*For the class:*
    plant with a taproot

## Background Information
The root is one of the first parts of a plant that starts to grow. As the embryo develops, the root pushes into the soil. At the tip of each root is a protective cap of cells that shields the root as it pushes through the soil.

The roots are perhaps the least seen of any of the plants parts, but they can extend over a larger area than the parts above ground. The *fibrous root system*, evident in grasses and weeds, has a mass of branching roots spreading in all directions. A *taproot system*, exemplified by carrots, has one large root that grows straight down.

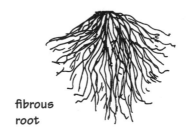

fibrous
root

taproot

Roots have several functions. They anchor the plant to the ground and help keep it upright. They can store food for the plant to use. Roots also absorb the nutrients needed for plant growth. Water and minerals are taken in through the fine root hairs that grow near the tips. In addition, roots help prevent the erosion of soil by wind and water.

## Management

1. To maximize up-close, hands-on observations, divide the class into groups of five or six students. Each group will need a plant with fibrous roots.
2. Survey the playground for potential weed plants (fibrous roots). If suitable ones are not available, obtain a couple of small grass plants from a nursery. For a taproot plant, obtain a carrot or dig up a dandelion. Leave it in a moist area until rootlets start to grow.

## Procedure

*Part One*

1. Distribute the observation sheet, rulers, and digging tools. Take the class outside and instruct each group to find a weed plant.
2. Invite students to carefully study the weed, sketch and measure the part above ground (step 2), and draw the predicted underground root system (step 3).
3. Tell students to carefully dig up the weed—keeping the root system intact—and soak the roots in water to remove the soil. Have them draw and measure the actual root system in the lower part of step 2 and compare it with their prediction.
4. Instruct students to lay their plants on a newspaper and gently spread the roots, stems, and leaves. Have them draw one circle around the roots and another circle around the part of the plant that was above ground. How do the two circles compare? How else does the plant compare with its roots?
5. If you have several taproot plants, distribute one to each group. If you have one, display its root system. Have students observe the small branch roots that grow from the main taproot. Ask students to compare the fibrous root system with the taproot system.

*Part Two*

1. To observe tiny root hairs, germinate radish seeds. Direct groups to fold a paper towel so it will fit inside a plastic bag. Have them attach two-sided tape to the towel, press four radish seeds on the tape, and place in the bag with the seeds facing toward the outside.
2. To dampen the towel, instruct students to add water to the plastic bag, keeping the water level below the seeds. After the bag is sealed, place in a warm area of the room and wait several days for the roots to form. Do not open the bag.
3. Have students examine the fuzzy area near the tip of each root with a hands lens. Tell them to draw their observations on the sheet.
4. Direct students to open the bag and observe the root hairs collapsing when exposed to air.

## Connecting Learning

1. What is the purpose of roots? [anchor plant, absorb water and minerals for the plant to grow, sometimes store food for plant]
2. Why is the root system of a plant so large? [The larger the surface area of the roots, the more water and minerals it is capable of absorbing.]
3. How does the fibrous root system compare with the taproot system? [fibrous—a mass of roots going in all directions; taproot—one large root growing straight down with smaller roots branching from it]
4. What is the white fuzz that appears on the roots of seeds? [root hairs] What do they do for the plant? [absorb water and minerals]
5. How do roots help with erosion control? [helps prevent soil from being blown away by wind or carried away by water]
6. What damage can roots do? [push up sidewalks, get into water pipes, etc.]
7. How do humans use roots? [We use some as food—carrots, radishes, beets, and sweet potatoes. See *Plant Structure Facts* for other uses.]
8. What are you wondering now?

## Extensions

1. Compare the mass of the fibrous root system with the mass of the plant above ground. Does the relationship vary during plant's stages of life? Is there a difference between annuals and perennials? Try a carrot or turnip with the top attached.
2. Measure the longest root of a grass or weed (fibrous root) plant and compare it to the length of the stem.
3. Grow alfalfa or bean seeds on a damp towel. Observe the root system as it grows.
4. Put a cutting of ivy, philodendron, or coleus in a transparent glass of water. Observe how the new roots develop.
5. Grow a sweet potato vine in water. Which grows first—the new sprouts on the potato or the root system?

## Curriculum Correlation

*Social Studies*

Have students research and report on the use of roots for food. Challenge them to find some unusual roots that are used for food (taro root, horseradish, ginger).

\* Reprinted with permission from *Principles and Standards for School Mathematics,* 2000 by the National Council of Teachers of Mathematics. All rights reserved.

© 2005 AIMS Education Foundation

# DOWN UNDER

## Key Question

What does a plant's root system look like?

## Learning Goal

**Students will:**

- observe the root system of a plant and compare it with the growth above ground.

# DOWN UNDER

## Part One

1. Find a weed to observe. Imagine what it looks like under the ground.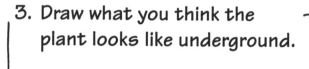

2. Sketch and measure the weed above the ground.

3. Draw what you think the plant looks like underground.

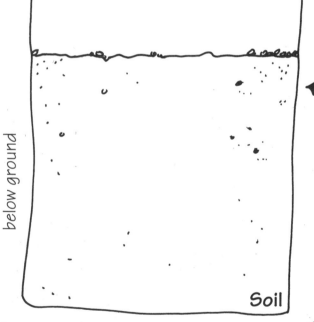

*above ground*

*below ground*

Soil

4. Carefully dig up the weed. Remove the soil. Sketch and measure the roots.

5. How does the plant compare with its roots?

## Part Two

Germinate radish seeds. Observe and draw the roots.

1. What is the purpose of roots?

2. Why is the root system of a plant so large?

3. How does the fibrous root system compare with the taproot system?

4. What is the white fuzz that appears on the roots of seeds? What do they do for the plant?

5. How do roots help with erosion control?

6. What damage can roots do?

7. How do humans use roots?

8. What are you wondering now?

© 2005 AIMS Education Foundation

# Herb and Woody

## Topic
Plant stems

## Key Questions
1. How do woody and herbaceous stems compare?
2. How are nutrients (food, water, and minerals) transported in plants?

## Learning Goals
Students will:
- compare and contrast woody and herbaceous stems, and
- observe the stem as a transport system.

## Guiding Documents
*Project 2061 Benchmark*
- *Scientific investigations may take many different forms, including observing what things are like or what is happening somewhere, collecting specimens for analysis, and doing experiments. Investigations can focus on physical, biological, and social questions.*

*NRC Standards*
- *Employ simple equipment and tools to gather data and extend the senses.*
- *Simple instruments, such as magnifiers, thermometers, and rulers, provide more information than scientists obtain using only their senses.*
- *Each plant or animal has different structures that serve different functions in growth, survival, and reproduction. For example, humans have distinct body structures for walking, holding, seeing, and talking.*

## Science
Life science
  botany
    stems
    transport system

## Integrated Processes
Observing
Collecting and recording data
Comparing and contrasting
Classifying
Inferring

## Materials
*For each group:*
  woody and herbaceous stems (see *Management 1*)
  hand lens
  celery stalk with leaves
  tall plastic cup
  water
  red food coloring
  serrated knife

## Background Information
The main functions of a stem are to support leaves and flowers and to transport water, minerals, and food between the roots and the leaves. Water and minerals are absorbed through the roots and move up through the tube-like tissue (xylem) in the roots and stems to the leaves. The food sugar made in the leaves moves down through food-conducting tissue (phloem) in the stem to other parts of the plant.

There are basically two kinds of stems—woody and herbaceous. *Woody stems* are hard, brown, and rigid. They grow larger in diameter each year; some live hundreds of years. Woody-stemmed plants are usually large and include trees and shrubs.

*Herbaceous stems* are soft, green, and flexible. Plants with herbaceous stems usually live just one growing season and produce only small-sized plants. Grasses, beans, corn, and lilies have herbaceous stems.

The xylem and phloem tubes of herbaceous stems are bundled. The bundles are scattered throughout the stem in monocots; they form a circular pattern in dicots. In contrast, the tubes in woody stems are separated—the xylem tubes in the sapwood and the phloem tubes in the inner bark.

People use stems for food. Asparagus, rhubarb, bamboo shoots, and green onions are stems. Cane sugar comes from sugar cane; maple sugar comes from the sap of maple trees when their trunks have been tapped.

Woody stems produce wood for buildings, furniture, paper, and other products. Cork, rubber, and linen all come from woody or herbaceous stems.

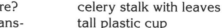

## Management

1. Collect a variety of herbaceous (geranium, tomato, lily, tomato, grass) and woody (trees, shrubs) stems.
2. Provide fresh stalks of celery with a few leaves attached. Slightly wilted celery will take up water faster than crisp celery.
3. Divide the class into small groups.

## Procedure

*Part One: Classification*

1. Introduce the words, herbaceous and woody. Ask the first *Key Question,* "How do woody and herbaceous stems compare?"
2. Distribute a variety of stems and have students separate them into the two groups.
3. Instruct groups to choose one herbaceous stem and one woody stem to observe. Have them examine the stems with a hand lens, make a sketch of each stem, and write a description including color, size, texture, smell, measurements, and bark.
4. Have students cut the end of the stem, study the cross section, and add to the description.
5. Ask students to compare and contrast the two stems on another piece of paper.

*Part Two: Transport system*

1. Ask the second *Key Question,* "How are nutrients (food, water, and minerals) transported in plants?" Explain that stems help carry water and minerals from the roots to the leaves and food made in the leaves to the rest of the plant. They will use celery to observe how water moves through stems.
2. Have students add about 10 drops of food coloring to a cup half-full of water, enough to make the water a dark color.
3. With a serrated knife, have students make a fresh cut across the base of the celery stalk and put the stalk in the colored water.
4. Let the celery stand in the water for 24 hours; invite students to check for any changes every half-hour or so.
5. After 24 hours, have students observe and discuss changes in the stem and leaves.
6. To take a closer look, ask students to remove the stem from the water and cut crosswise near the bottom. Tell them to sketch what they see with their eyes, and then what they see with a hand lens.
7. Direct students to use both hands to snap the celery in half. Have them remove the long, colored xylem tubes, observe them with a microscope, and sketch.

## Connecting Learning

*Part One: Classification*

1. How are herbaceous and woody stems different?
2. Is a tree trunk woody or herbaceous? [woody] Explain.

*Part Two: Transport system*

1. What are the functions of stems? [supports flowers and leaves, pathways for water and food between roots and leaves]
2. What does it mean to transport something? What evidence do you have that the celery's xylem tubes transported something? [The xylem tubes carried the colored water up the stem to the leaves; both the tubes and the leaves turned red.]
3. What are you wondering now?

## Extensions

1. Put a geranium stalk or white flowers such as a daisy, carnation, or lily in colored water. Observe what happens.
2. Try other liquids such as apple juice, coffee, or tea. Does the kind of liquid make a difference in the way it rises in the stem?
3. Use a leafy branch of beech, magnolia, or eucalyptus. Mix one-half cup glycerine with one cup of hot water; allow to cool. Crush the bottom one centimeter of the stems and put them in the glycerine mixture. Let stand until the leaves turn brown—a few days to a few weeks.

## Curriculum Correlation

*Literacy*

Have students research ways people have made use of plant stems. Some of these uses include linen, medicines, turpentine, and food.

# Herb and Woody

## Key Questions

1. How do woody and herbaceous stems compare?

2. How are nutrients (food, water, and minerals) transported in plants?

## Learning Goals

### Students will:

- compare and contrast woody and herbaceous stems, and

- observe the stem as a transport system.

 © 2005 AIMS Education Foundation

# Herb and Woody

### Stems support leaves and flowers.

**A.** **Observe:** Find two kinds of stems. Record observations, including measurements.

## Herbaceous Stem (celery, grasses, lilies, clover)

| Sketch | Description: |
|--------|--------------|
|        |              |
|        |              |
|        |              |
|        |              |
|        |              |
|        |              |
|        |              |

## Woody Stem (trees and shrubs)

| Sketch | Description: |
|--------|--------------|
|        |              |
|        |              |
|        |              |
|        |              |
|        |              |
|        |              |
|        |              |

**B.** **Compare:** Use your notes to write a summary. Compare and contrast the stems you observed.

# Herb and Woody

## How does a plant get water to the leaves?

### You will need:
- fresh celery stalk with leaves
- cup of water
- red food coloring
- hand lens
- microscope

## Do this:

1. Stems transport water from the soil to all parts of a plant through tubes called xylem. To see the xylem, place the stalk of celery in a cup of water to which you've added some food coloring.

2. Leave the celery in the water for several hours, but watch for changes every half-hour or so.

3. When you see a lot of color in the leaves, take the celery out of the water.

4. Cut a thin slice across the stem. Observe with your eyes and a hand lens. Sketch.

5. Use both hands to break the celery in half. Remove the long, colored tubes. Observe the tubes and stalk with a microscope.

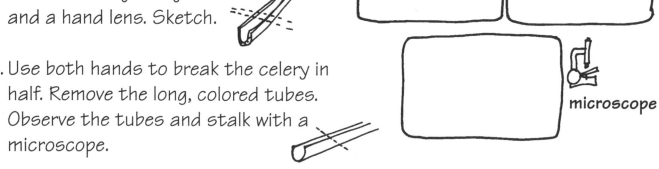

eyes

hand lens

microscope

6. These "strings" are the xylem tubes. They are part of the transport system of the plant. What evidence do you have that they transported something?

# Herb and Woody

**CONNECTING LEARNING**

## Part One

1. How are herbaceous and woody stems different?

2. Is a tree trunk woody or herbaceous? Explain.

## Part Two

1. What are the functions of stems?

2. What does it mean to transport something? What evidence do you have that the celery's xylem tubes transported something?

3. What are you wondering now?

# A Twig's Story

**Topic**
Tree twigs

**Key Questions**
1. How can twigs be used to identify trees?
2. How can the age of a twig be determined?

**Learning Goal**
Students will learn about growth patterns of tree branches by observing twigs.

**Guiding Documents**
*Project 2061 Benchmark*
- *Scientific investigations may take many different forms, including observing what things are like or what is happening somewhere, collecting specimens for analysis, and doing experiments. Investigations can focus on physical, biological, and social questions.*

*NRC Standards*
- *Employ simple equipment and tools to gather data and extend the senses.*
- *Simple instruments, such as magnifiers, thermometers, and rulers, provide more information than scientists obtain using only their senses.*
- *Each plant or animal has different structures that serve different functions in growth, survival, and reproduction. For example, humans have distinct body structures for walking, holding, seeing, and talking.*

**Science**
Life science
    botany
        trees

**Integrated Processes**
Observing
Comparing and contrasting
Collecting and recording data
Generalizing

**Materials**
*For each student or group:*
    tree twigs collected before spring growth
        (walnut, horse chestnut, oak, pecan, apple, etc.)
    hand lens
    metric tape

*For the class:*
    small head of red cabbage
    knife
    overhead transparency of the twig diagram

**Background Information**
A tree puts on new growth at the tip of each branch. In deciduous trees (trees that lose their leaves), new growth buds form at the end of the stems during the summer. These buds contain the cells for the new stems and leaves that grow quickly once the weather warms in spring.

Trees have two kinds of buds. Twigs grow longer at the *terminal bud,* the bud on the end of a stem. It contains a tiny leafy green stem (shoot) and is wrapped in a protective covering of bud scales. *Lateral buds,* along the sides of the twigs, develop on the stem just above where the leaves are attached; they grow new side shoots or tiny branches off the main branch.

Trees can be identified, even after they have dropped their leaves, by examining the shape and arrangement of buds and leaf scars on twigs. Each type of tree has its own pattern of buds and scars. Maples, ashes, and dogwoods have *opposite buds* that grow in pairs across from each other. Poplars and birches have *alternate buds,* arranged alternately on the twigs. Some trees, such as oaks, have *clustered* or *whorled buds*—groups of buds at the tip of each twig.

The point where a twig begins its growth each season can be seen by the terminal bud scale scars that circle the stem. A year's growth can be measured from one terminal bud scale scar to the base of the next year's terminal bud. A twig's age can be determined by counting the number of terminal bud scale scars.

**Management**
1. Do this activity in winter or early spring, while trees are still dormant, so leafless twigs can be collected.
2. Gather twigs, preferably with terminal bud scale scars, from several kinds of trees. Trees with bigger buds and bud scars are easier to observe. If students are collecting the twigs, encourage them to pick only one small twig from each tree.
3. Since a terminal bud is so small, students will observe a cabbage head instead; it closely resembles the bud's internal structure.
4. To acquaint students with the structure of twigs, make an overhead transparency of the explanatory drawing.

## Procedure

1. Give each student a twig to observe with a hand lens.
2. Ask the two *Key Questions:* "How can twigs be used to identify trees?" and "How can the age of a twig be determined?" Give students time to discuss, observe, and propose some possible answers.
3. Use the transparency of the twig diagram to help students identify various parts of their twigs.
4. To locate a bud, have students look just above where each leaf was attached to the twig the year before. Help them identify and compare the terminal bud and lateral buds.

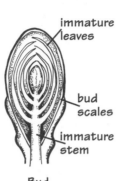

Bud

5. Distribute the observation page. Since the tiny terminal buds are difficult to dissect and observe, cut a small head of red cabbage (which has a similar structure) in half. Have students observe and draw the bud structure.
6. To determine the age of a twig, instruct students to locate and count the number of ring-like bud scars on their twigs, each representing one year. Explain that the terminal bud scale scar nearest the tip of the twig is where the terminal bud was last year. (Most likely, their twigs will have only one bud scale scar.)

7. Direct students to examine the leaf scars to determine whether their twigs have an alternate, opposite, or whorled leaf pattern. Leaf scars have the same pattern as buds.

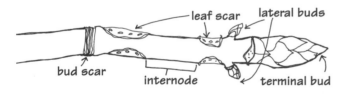

alternate          opposite          whorled

8. Ask students to draw their twigs, including the terminal bud, lateral buds, leaf scars, and bud scars.

9. Have students observe a leaf scar with a hands lens, then draw it and its bundle scars. Explain that the bundle scars are the water-conducting (xylem) and food-conducting (phloem) tissues.

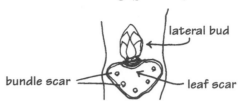

10. Instruct students to measure and record the lengths of the twig, twig growth (between terminal bud scars), internode (between leaf scars), and terminal bud.
11. Have students count and record the numbers of leaf scars, lateral buds (above last year's terminal bud scale scar), and terminal bud scars.
12. For assessment, revisit the two *Key Questions.*

## Connecting Learning

1. What surprised you about the twigs?
2. Describe the terminal bud. Do all twigs have a terminal bud?
3. How does the terminal bud compare with the lateral buds? [The terminal bud is larger.]
4. Why are the growths called terminal buds and lateral buds?
5. What is the age of your twig? How do you know?
6. How many centimeters did your twig grow last year?
7. How many leaves had grown on your twig? How are they arranged?
8. How are lateral buds related to leaf scars? [The lateral buds grow just above the leaf scars and in the same arrangement.]
9. What are you wondering now?

## Extensions

1. Use twigs from several different trees to test students' ability to identify the twigs' parts.
2. Give students twigs from two different trees and *A Tale of Two Twigs.* Have them sketch the twigs and compare the twigs' characteristics.
3. Keep twigs from several different trees. When the same kind of trees start to leaf out in spring and summer, collect some leafy twigs for students to match with the dormant twigs.

## Curriculum Correlation

*Literacy*

Write *A Twig's Story* about how a twig grows from spring until fall.

\* Reprinted with permission from *Principles and Standards for School Mathematics,* 2000 by the National Council of Teachers of Mathematics. All rights reserved.

# A Twig's Story

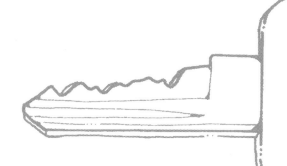

## Key Questions

1. How can twigs be used to identify trees?

2. How can the age of a twig be determined?

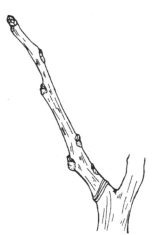

## Learning Goal

### Students will:

- learn about growth patterns of tree branches by observing twigs.

© 2005 AIMS Education Foundation

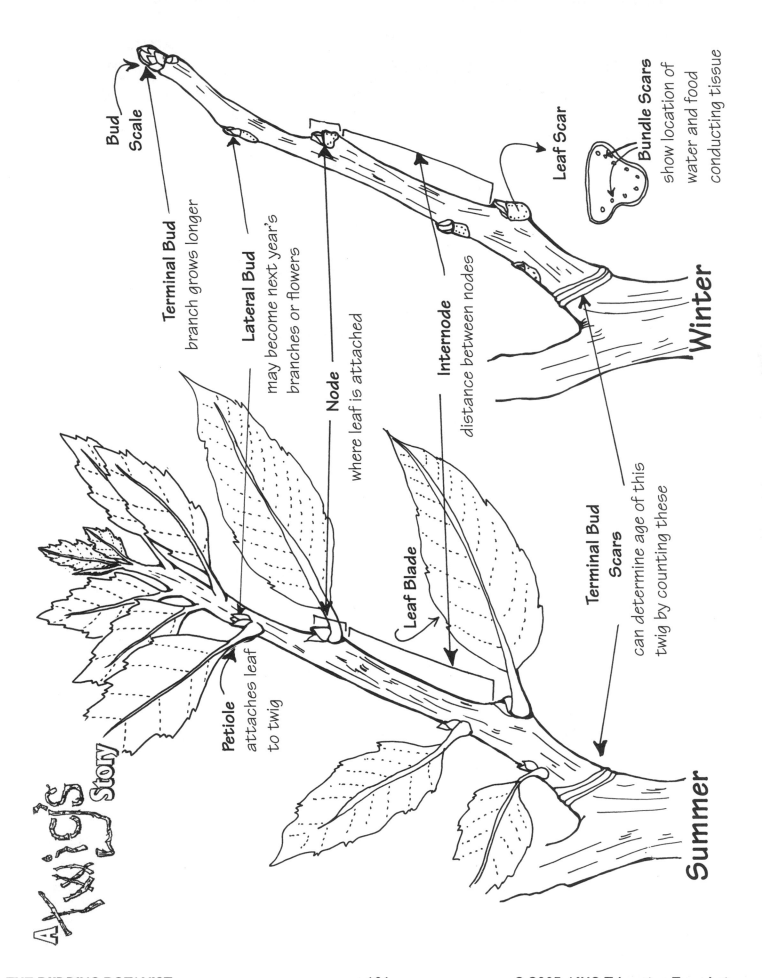

# A Twig's Story

**Bud Scale**

**Terminal Bud**
branch grows longer

**Lateral Bud**
may become next year's branches or flowers

**Node**
where leaf is attached

**Internode**
distance between nodes

**Leaf Scar**

**Bundle Scars**
show location of water and food conducting tissue

**Petiole**
attaches leaf to twig

**Leaf Blade**

**Terminal Bud Scars**
can determine age of this twig by counting these

**Winter**

**Summer**

# A Twig's Story

**Collect** a twig in winter or spring, while trees are still dormant.

**Observe** and draw your twig.

Identify: terminal bud
lateral buds
nodes
bundle scars

Terminal bud

**Measure**

Length of twig: _____ cm

Length of twig growth (1 year): _____ cm

Length of internode: _____ cm

Length of terminal bud: _____ cm

Twig

A leaf scar with bundle scars

**Count**

# of leaf scars: _____

# of lateral buds: _____

# of terminal bud scars: _____

**Tell** your twig's story:

Sketch two different twigs, including the buds and scars.

Compare and contrast the two twigs, including number of bud scars, age of twig, leaf pattern, etc.

# A Twig's Story

CONNECTING LEARNING

1.  What surprised you about the twigs?

2.  Describe the terminal bud. Do all twigs have a terminal bud?

3.  How does the terminal bud compare with the lateral buds?

4.  Why are the growths called terminal and lateral buds?

5.  What is the age of your twig? How do you know?

6.  How many centimeters did your twig grow last year?

7.  How many leaves had grown on your twig? How are they arranged?

8.  How are lateral buds related to leaf scars?

9.  What are you wondering now?

# Leaf Facts

## Function

The leaf is the main food-making part of almost all plants. Leaves work like tiny food factories in a process called *photosynthesis*. The

green chlorophyll in the chloroplasts of leaves uses energy from sunlight, water from the soil, and carbon dioxide from the air to make a food substance called glucose. Plants store the glucose in their fruits, roots, seeds, stems, and even in the leaves themselves. Oxygen, a by-product of photosynthesis, is released into the air. All living organisms depend on oxygen for survival.

When the plant needs food, *respiration* breaks down the glucose. This releases energy for the plant to grow, reproduce, and make repairs. Respiration is the opposite of photosynthesis. Photosynthesis makes food; respiration breaks down food. Photosynthesis happens during daylight, while respiration goes on day and night. Respiration helps plants survive the winters and at night.

Water enters the plant through the roots and travels up the xylem tubes in plant stems to the leaves. In the process of *transpiration,* most of this water evaporates into the air as water vapor, mainly through the stomata or tiny openings in the leaves. This loss of water pulls up more water from the roots.

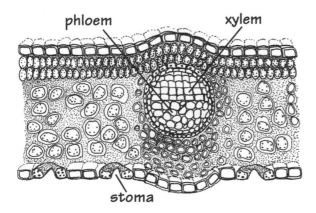

Each leaf has two distinct sides. The upper side is usually dark and waxy; the underside shows the veins more clearly. The veins are the leaf's distribution system, carrying water and nutrients throughout the leaf. Counting both sides of the leaves, an established tree has an enormous leaf surface.

## Structure

Leaves vary greatly in appearance and shape. A blade of grass, a pine needle, a fern frond, a cactus thorn, and an oak leaf—all are leaves. Leaves may be large or small, narrow or wide, long or short. They may have smooth, saw-toothed, or wavy edges.

Some are thickened for water storage. Some leaves are divided into several leaflets. Leaves are used to identify plants because of their distinctive nature.

Most leaves have two parts, the blade and the petiole. The *blade* is the broad, flat part of a leaf that provides a large, exposed surface to collect solar energy. The *petiole* is the stalk of the leaf that joins the blade to the stem. The petiole supports the blade and turns it towards the sun. The midrib is the central vein of the leaf.

Buds develop at the base of leaves, just above where the leaves are attached to the stem. The growth tissue at these places, called nodes, can become new leaves, flowers, or stems.

Leaves may be either simple or compound. A *simple leaf* consists of one petiole and one blade. It is a single, intact structure, even though the edge may be indented by lobes or teeth. Trees (oak, maple, and elm) and grasses are among the many plants that have simple leaves.

A *compound leaf* has one petiole with many leaflets. In pinnately compound leaves, leaflets are attached in pairs along a central stalk (rachis) extending from the petiole. In palmately compound leaves, all of the leaflets are attached to the petiole at one point.

Scientists divide leaves into two large groups, *broad* leaves and *needle-like* leaves. Angiosperms, or flowering plants, usually have flat, wide leaves. Gymnosperms, such as pines, typically have needle-like leaves.

Broad leaves are classified by their vein patterns. Long, slender, flat leaves—most often found on monocots—usually have a *parallel* vein pattern. The larger veins run parallel to one another from the leaf stem to the blade tip. Small cross veins connect the large veins. Corn, wheat, lilies, onions, and lawn grasses have parallel venation.

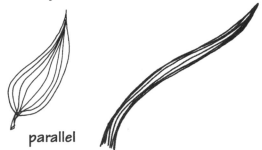
parallel

Wide, flat leaves—commonly found on dicots—usually have a *netted* vein pattern in which several large veins are connected by many smaller ones. Netted veins can have either a pinnate or a palmate pattern. In *pinnately* veined leaves, such as those of elm, walnut, and birch trees, the main vein or midrib has secondary veins branching from it like a feather. *Palmately* veined leaves, such as those of maple, sycamore, and liquidambar trees, have several main veins of similar size extending from a common point at the base of the blade; the vein pattern resembles the palm of your hand.

pinnate

palmate

The leaves on gymnosperms are most often needle-like; they are found on firs, pines, spruces, and most other cone-bearing trees and shrubs. Needle leaves can be divided into two groups—needles attached *singly* to a stem (spruces and firs) and needles attached in *bundles* of two, three, or five (pines). Needle leaves are so small that they usually have only one vein that runs through the center of the leaf. Scale-like leaves are found on a few kinds of cone-bearing plants like cedars and junipers.

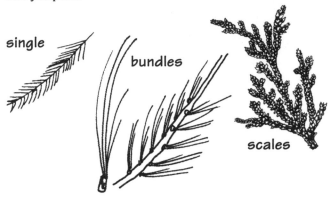
single
bundles
scales

# Leafy Facts

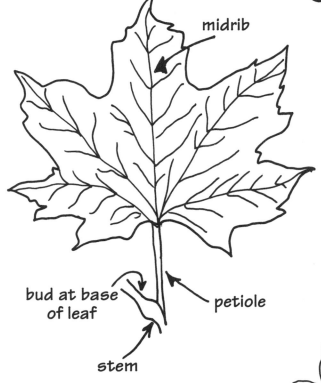

midrib

bud at base
of leaf

petiole

stem

## Simple Leaf

The broad, flat part of a leaf is called the blade. The blade is connected to the stem by the petiole. The petiole supports the blade and turns it towards the sun. The bud grows at the base of the leaf. The midrib is the central stalk of the leaf.

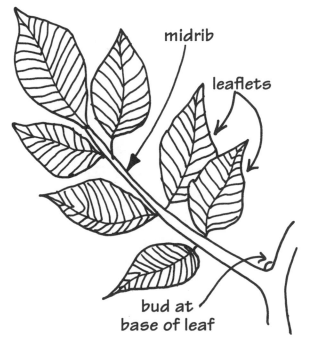

midrib

leaflets

bud at
base of leaf

## Compound Leaf

In some plants, the blades are divided into a number of small leaves called leaflets. A compound leaf has a number of leaflets arranged in two rows facing each other along the midrib. One leaflet may grow at the tip of the midrib of some compound leaves. Buds always appear at the base of the leaf, never at the base of the leaflets.

© 2005 AIMS Education Foundation

# More Leafy Facts

A blade of grass, a pine needle, a fern frond, and a maple leaf are all leaves. Most leaves need light, air, and water. Leaves contain green cells to make food for the entire plant.

Leaves look very different, however. Every plant has its own distinctive kind of leaf. Leaves help us identify plants like fingerprints identify people.

Almost all other leaves can be grouped into **broad** leaves. Broad leaves can be further classified by their pattern of veins.

The **branched**, or webbed group, can be classified into two groups—pinnate (featherlike) or palmate (fanlike).

The veins in a **palmate** leaf fan out from the petiole and form a network of smaller veins.

In palms, grasses, and other plants, the veins run **parallel** to one another from the petiole to blade tip.

In the **pinnate** group, the veins branch out from the midrib like barbs of a feather.

**Needle-like** leaves can be divided into two groups.

Others have needles attached in **bundles** of two, three, or four.

Needles can be attached **singly** to a stem.

© 2005 AIMS Education Foundation

## Topic
Leaf classification

## Key Question
What structures help us classify leaves?

## Learning Goals
Students will:
- make observations of various leaf structures, and
- use these structures to classify leaves.

## Guiding Documents
*Project 2061 Benchmarks*
- *A great variety of kinds of living things can be sorted into groups in many ways using various features to decide which things belong to which group.*
- *Features used for grouping depend on the purpose of the grouping.*

*NRC Standards*
- *Objects have many observable properties, including size, weight, shape, color, temperature, and the ability to react with other substances. Those properties can be measured using tools, such as rulers, balances, and thermometers.*
- *Each plant or animal has different structures that serve different functions in growth, survival, and reproduction. For example, humans have distinct body structures for walking, holding, seeing, and talking.*

*NTCM Standards 2000\**
- *Understand such attributes as length, area, weight, volume, and size of angle and select the appropriate type of unit for measuring each attribute*
- *Select and apply appropriate standard units and tools to measure length, area, volume, weight, time, temperature, and the size of angles*

## Math
Measurement
length
area

## Science
Life science
botany
plant structures

## Integrated Processes
Observing
Comparing and contrasting
Collecting and recording data
Classifying

## Materials
*For each group:*
10 leaves
metric rulers
sticky dots

## Background Information
See *Leaf Facts, Leafy Facts,* and *More Leafy Facts.*

## Management
1. Bring in samples of simple, compound, pinnate, palmate, and parallel-veined leaves.
2. After *Part One*, students can collect leaves from their yards or neighborhood. Instruct them to collect only one leaf per plant.
3. Keep leaves fresh overnight by placing them in reclosable plastic bags.
4. Make transparencies of the two *Leafy Facts* sheets.

## Procedure
*Part One: Gathering information*
1. Pass around samples of simple and compound leaves, followed by pinnate, palmate, and parallel-veined leaves.
2. On chart paper or an overhead transparency, have the class brainstorm a list of attributes of the sample leaves. Discuss and record ideas on the function of leaves.
3. Use the overhead transparencies of *Leafy Facts* to help students identify the different kinds of leaves.
4. Assign students to collect a variety of leaves—keeping in mind the types of leaves just discussed—and bring them to school the next day. Caution them to bring all of a compound leaf, not just the leaflets.

*Part Two: Observing and measuring*
1. Review the lists of attributes and functions that were generated during *Part One*.
2. Distribute the first activity sheet. Have each student choose one leaf and trace it on the 1-cm grid. Tell them to record the shape, color, and texture.

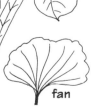

heart-shaped

long, pointed

fan

3. Instruct students to observe the vein structure in their leaves by a) holding them up to the light, and b) turning them over since the underside shows the structure better. What is the arrangement of the veins? Are they arranged in parallel veins as in a narrow leaf? Are they spreading out like the palm of a hand (palmate)? Are they arranged like the barbs of a feather (pinnate)?

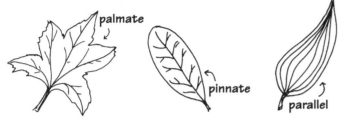

4. Tell students to draw the vein structure on the leaf tracing. Have them compare the veins of their leaves with those of other students. Explain that the veins are the pathways for food and water.
5. Direct students to look at the edges of their leaves. Are they smooth, lobed, or toothed?

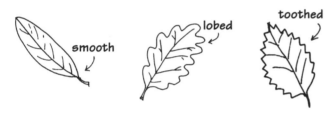

6. Have students measure the length and width of their leaves using a measuring tape or by counting on the grid.
7. Instruct students to figure the surface area by counting the number of squares the leaf covers on the grid.
8. Invite students to write an official description of their leaves using the properties they have observed and a variety of adjectives such as pointed, velvety, smooth, long, and jagged.

*Part Three: Comparing*
1. Guide students in forming teams of four botanists. Instruct each team to choose 10 different leaves. Using sticky dots, have them label each leaf with a number.
2. Give teams the second activity sheet. Have them record the leaves' attributes on the chart.

3. Tell students to choose an attribute, group the leaves, and explain the grouping.
   *Sample groups*
   Veins: palmate, pinnate, parallel
   Edges: toothed, lobed, serrated, smooth
   Texture: rough, smooth, velvety, slick, waxy, sticky
   Color: light green, dark green, red, yellow
   Shape: oval, round, heart, fan, long, pointed
4. Repeat with another attribute.
5. Have each team challenge another student to match leaves and numbers without looking at the labels.

**Connecting Learning**
1. What structures do many leaves have in common? [blade, petiole]
2. What is a petiole? [stem-like part that joins the blade to the stem] Which of your leaves have a petiole attached?
3. What is the purpose of veins? [They transport nutrients throughout the leaves.]
4. How does the vein structure of a palmate and pinnate leaf compare?
5. In your sample, what was the most common kind of _____? (name an attribute)
6. What are you wondering now?

**Extensions**
1. Use fabric paint and make leaf prints on muslin cloth or T-shirts (see *Leaf Printing*). By applying paint to the underside of most leaves, you will create a print with elaborate detail of the vein structure.
2. Do leaf rubbings to show shape, edge, and vein structure. Place thin paper over a leaf and rub back and forth with a crayon.
3. Preserve leaves by pressing them between layers of absorbent paper and sticking them in the pages of thick books. Display, possibly as a leaf mobile.
4. Use two or more leaf attributes to make Venn diagrams.

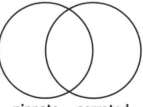

pinnate   serrated

*   Reprinted with permission from *Principles and Standards for School Mathematics, 2000* by the National Council of Teachers of Mathematics. All rights reserved.

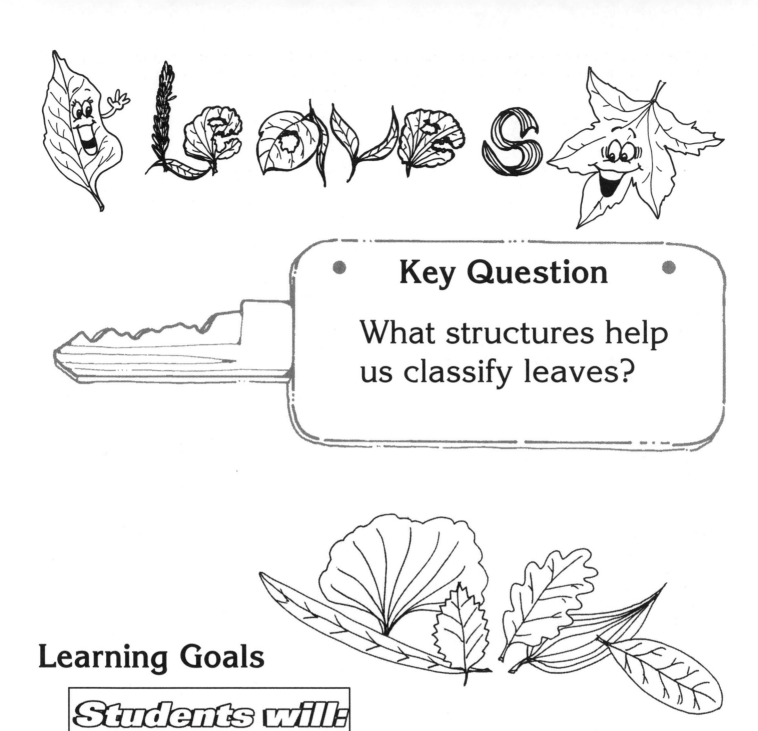

# Leaves

## Key Question

What structures help us classify leaves?

## Learning Goals

### Students will:

- make observations of various leaf structures, and

- use these structures to classify leaves.

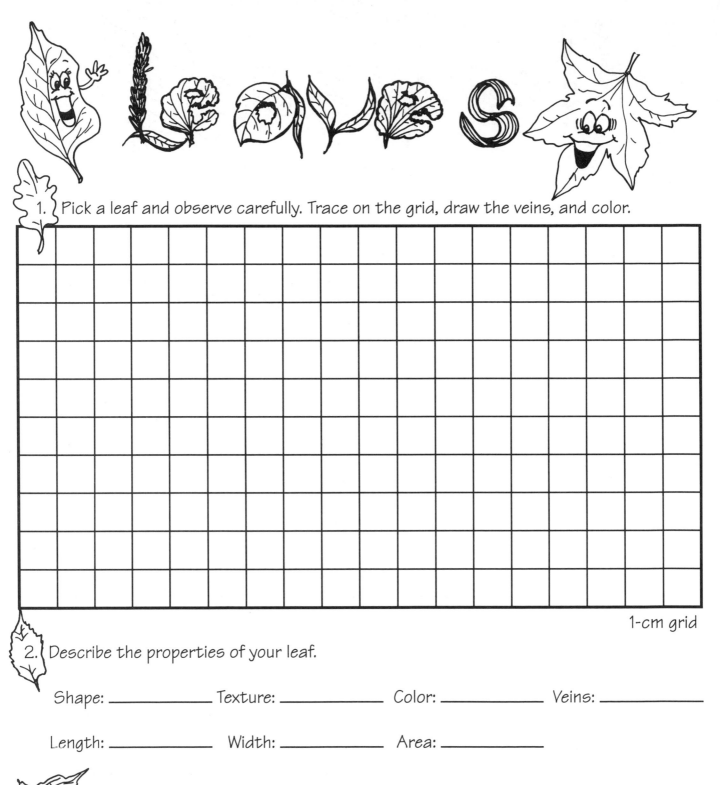

**1.** Pick a leaf and observe carefully. Trace on the grid, draw the veins, and color.

1-cm grid

**2.** Describe the properties of your leaf.

Shape: _____  Texture: _____  Color: _____  Veins: _____

Length: _____  Width: _____  Area: _____

**3.** Describe your leaf so someone else can identify it.

1. Form a team of botanists to study leaves. Choose 10 different leaves and label them 1 to 10.
2. Record the attributes of the leaves.

| Leaf # | Veins | Edges | Texture | Color | Shape |
|--------|-------|-------|---------|-------|-------|
| 1 | | | | | |
| 2 | | | | | |
| 3 | | | | | |
| 4 | | | | | |
| 5 | | | | | |
| 6 | | | | | |
| 7 | | | | | |
| 8 | | | | | |
| 9 | | | | | |
| 10 | | | | | |

3. Group the leaves by one attribute. Explain. Repeat with other attributes.

          © 2005 AIMS Education Foundation

# LEAVES

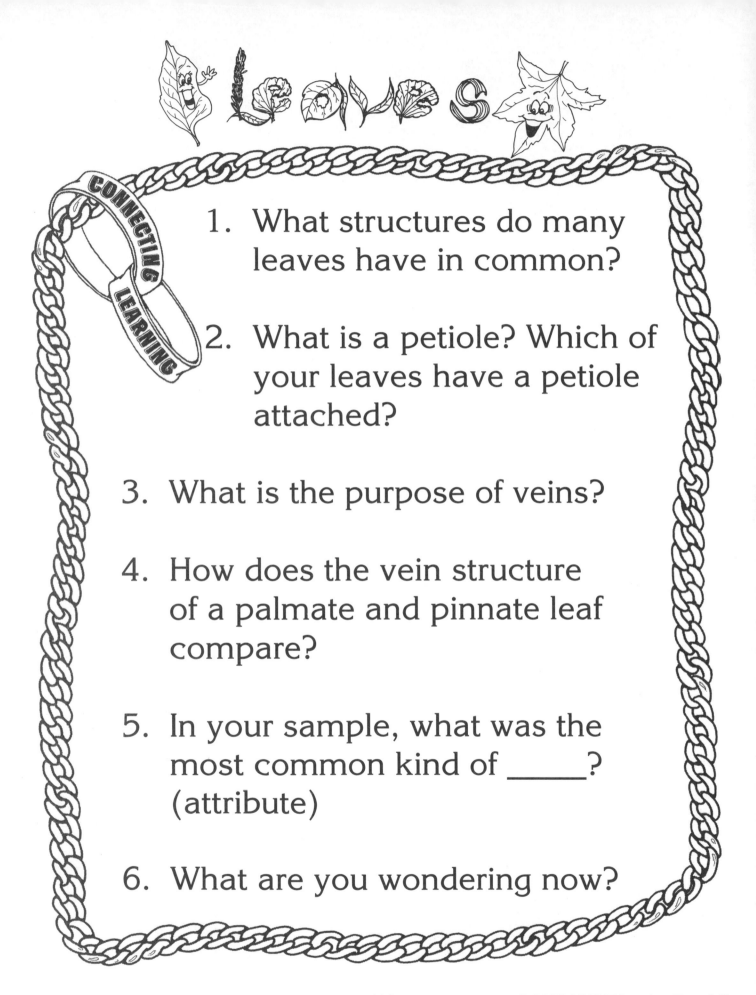

1. What structures do many leaves have in common?

2. What is a petiole? Which of your leaves have a petiole attached?

3. What is the purpose of veins?

4. How does the vein structure of a palmate and pinnate leaf compare?

5. In your sample, what was the most common kind of ____? (attribute)

6. What are you wondering now?

CONNECTING LEARNING

# Keyed to Leaves

## Topic
Leaf classification using a dichotomous key

## Key Question
How can we use a dichotomous key to classify leaves?

## Learning Goals
Students will:
- construct dichotomous keys, and
- use them to classify leaves.

## Guiding Documents
*Project 2061 Benchmarks*
- *A great variety of kinds of living things can be sorted into groups in many ways using various features to decide which things belong to which group.*
- *Features used for grouping depend on the purpose of the grouping.*

*NRC Standards*
- *Scientists use different kinds of investigations depending on the questions they are trying to answer. Types of investigations include describing objects, events, and organisms; classifying them; and doing a fair test (experimenting).*
- *Use appropriate tools and techniques to gather, analyze, and interpret data.*

## Math
Graphic organizer
   dichotomous key

## Science
Life science
   botany
      plant structures

## Integrated Processes
Observing
Comparing and contrasting
Collecting and recording data
Classifying

## Materials
*For each group:*
   10 leaves
   chart paper
   markers

## Background Information
Classification is often done with a dichotomous key. In using a dichotomous key, one chooses an attribute that divides a group into "haves" and "have nots." Using another attribute, the two subgroups are then divided again until each object being sorted is isolated. When complete, each object in the group is distinguished by a unique list of attributes. This method provides an efficient way of confirming what object of the group you have by asking only yes/no questions.

Dichotomous keys provide a vehicle by which students can compare and contrast items and better understand how they are unique. There are multiple ways for students to develop a key, depending on the attribute they choose for each division. The key can be designed to flow from top to bottom or from left to right.

For information on the attributes of leaves, see *Leaf Facts, Leafy Facts,* and *More Leafy Facts.*

## Management
1. Prior observations of leaf attributes (see the *Leaves* activity) are highly recommended.
2. It is assumed that students know how to make a dichotomous key. You may want to review the procedure before asking them to make one on chart paper. In order for students to become adept at reading dichotomous keys in various formats, you may want some groups to design theirs going left to right and other groups to design theirs going top to bottom.

## Procedure
1. Review vocabulary from prior leaf observations and write the words on the board. Inform students that they will be making dichotomous keys on which to identify and sort their leaves.
2. Review how a dichotomous key is constructed, if necessary. Tell groups that they will need to build a key that singles out all 10 of their leaves.
3. Distribute the chart paper. Encourage students to determine the attributes of the leaves and sort them into a dichotomous key.
4. Have students draw the dichotomous key on the chart paper, labeling each branch with the chosen attribute.
5. When the chart is finished, tell students to place their 10 leaves at the beginning. Have student groups rotate from chart to chart, sorting the leaves on the

dichotomous keys. Invite them to discuss any difficulties they had in making a determination and to come to a conclusion of how to clarify the sorting.

6. As an assessment, you may want students to use the pictures to complete the dichotomous key included in this activity.

## Connecting Learning

1. What are some of the different attributes of leaves? [shape, edge, color, vein structure, texture]
2. What kinds of shapes do you observe? [long, oval, round, heart, fan, pointed, etc.]
3. What is the difference in the vein structure between a parallel and a pinnate leaf?

4. What things do you have to remember when making a dichotomous key? [Leaves are always split into two groups, one group with a specific attribute (pinnate) and the other group without that attribute (not pinnate). Leaves continue to be split until there is only one left at the end of each series of attributes.]
5. Why is a dichotomous key useful? [It shows the unique set of attributes of a particular leaf.]
6. What are you wondering now?

## Extension

Use your group's dichotomous key to play the game, "I'm thinking of a leaf." Have other group members ask questions that can only be answered by a yes or no until the leaf is identified.

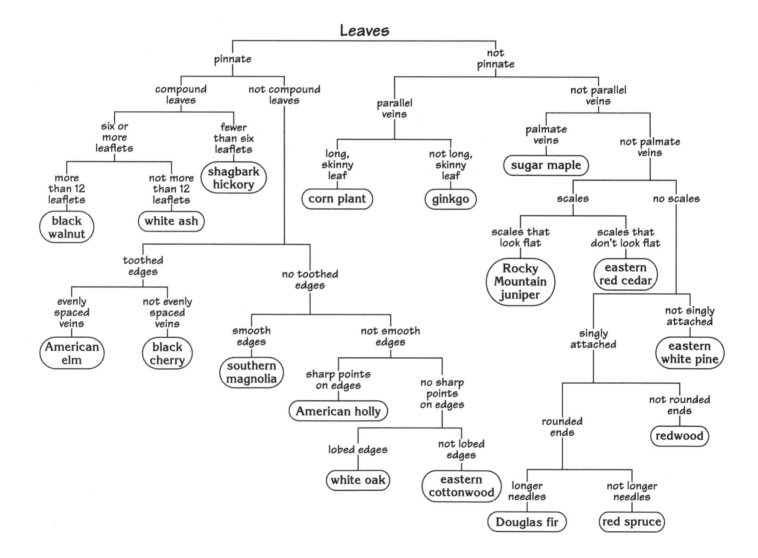

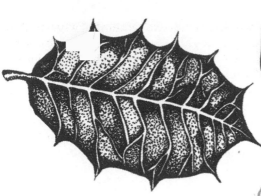

# Key**e**d to **L**eaves

## Key Question

How can we use a dichotomous key to classify leaves?

## Learning Goals

### Students will:

- construct dichotomous keys, and

- use them to classify leaves.

 © 2005 AIMS Education Foundation

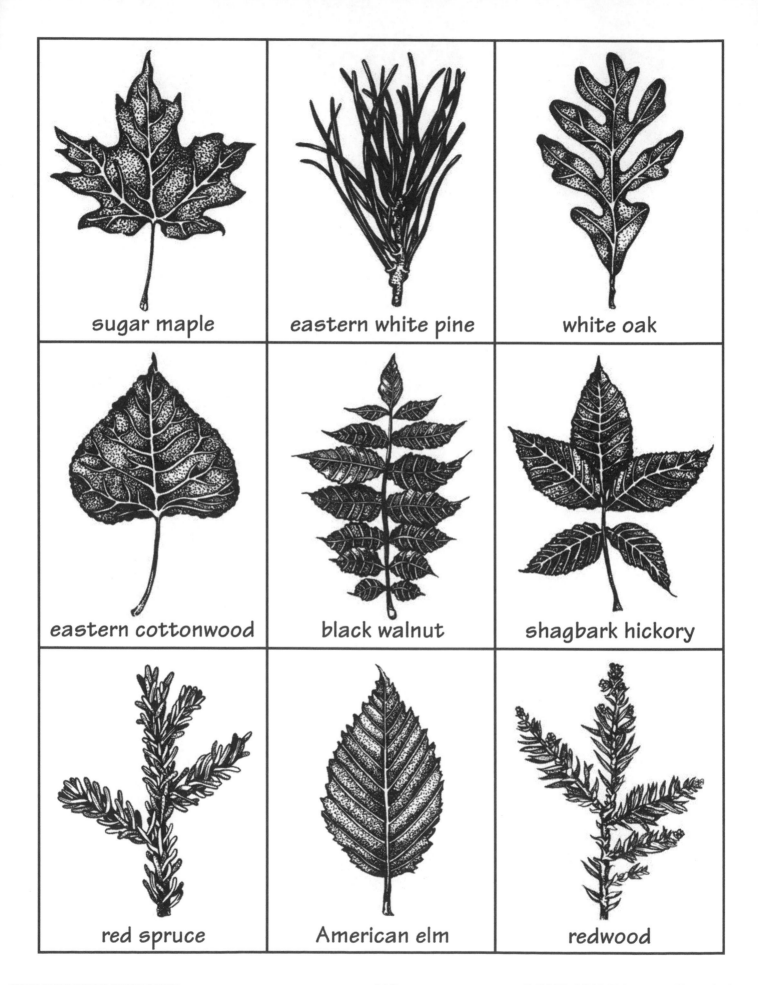

sugar maple

eastern white pine

white oak

eastern cottonwood

black walnut

shagbark hickory

red spruce

American elm

redwood

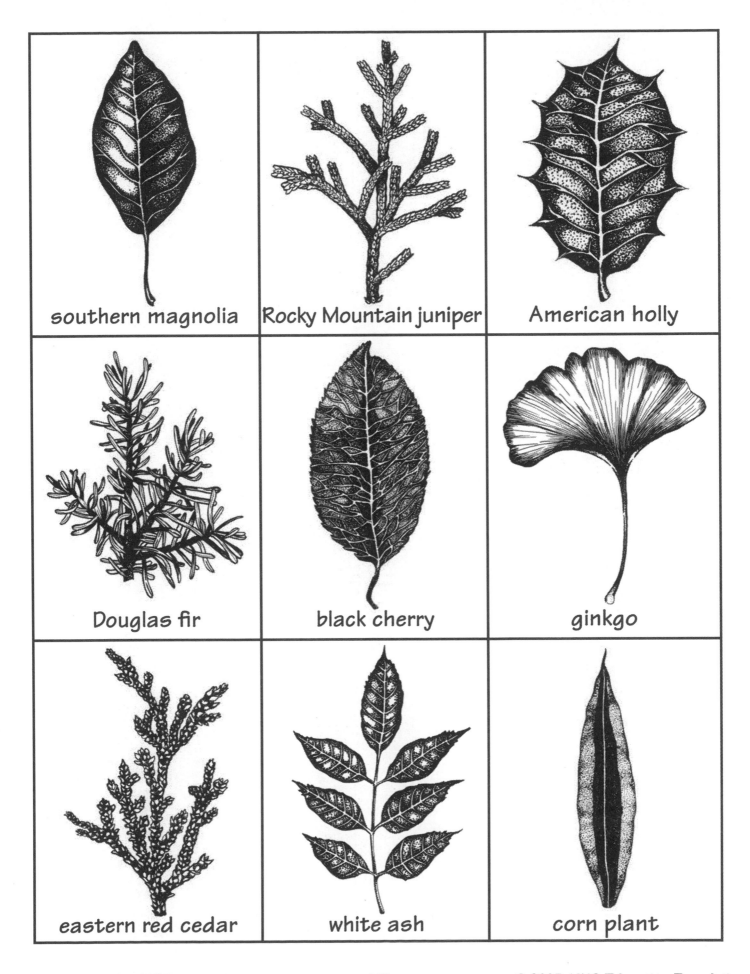

southern magnolia

Rocky Mountain juniper

American holly

Douglas fir

black cherry

ginkgo

eastern red cedar

white ash

corn plant

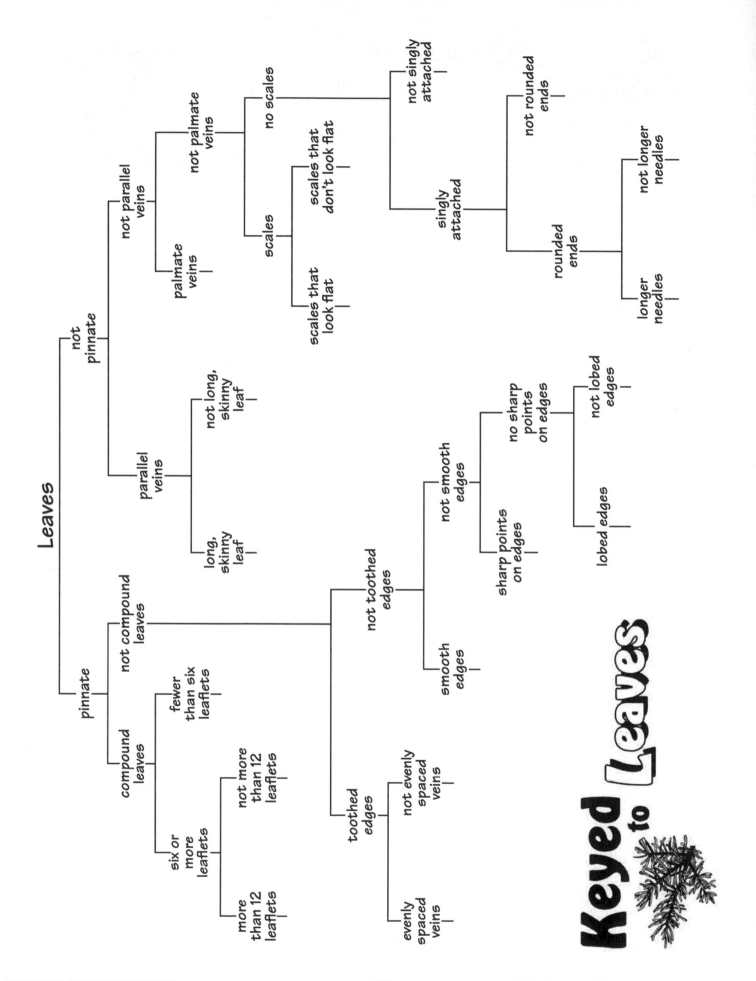

Leaves

pinnate
  compound leaves
    fewer than six leaflets
    six or more leaflets
      not more than 12 leaflets
      more than 12 leaflets
  not compound leaves
    toothed edges
      evenly spaced veins
      not evenly spaced veins
    not toothed edges
      smooth edges
      not smooth edges
        sharp points on edges
        no sharp points on edges
          lobed edges
          not lobed edges

not pinnate
  parallel veins
    long, skinny leaf
    not long, skinny leaf
  not parallel veins
    palmate veins
    not palmate veins
      scales
        scales that look flat
        scales that don't look flat
      no scales
        not singly attached
        singly attached
          not rounded ends
          rounded ends
            not longer needles
            longer needles

Keyed to Leaves

# Keyed to Leaves

CONNECTING LEARNING

1. What are some of the different attributes of leaves?

2. What kinds of shapes do you observe?

3. What is the difference in the vein structure between a parallel and a pinnate leaf?

4. What things do you have to remember when making a dichotomous key?

5. Why is a dichotomous key useful?

6. What are you wondering now?

# Leaf Printing

Leaf printing on T-shirts is a great opportunity to excite children of all ages about a unit on trees and plants. There are other benefits: it involves art with nature and science, it is almost foolproof, it builds great self esteem, and it provides opportunities to tell stories about special leaves printed on a particular shirt.

## Materials
Leaves (See *Management 1*)
Newspapers
4 2-oz bottles water-based acrylic paints
4 glass beakers (see *Management 4*)
Brushes or pieces of sponge
1/2 yard cotton knit fabric for practice
T-shirts
Iron

## Management
1. Gather fresh leaves (or dried, if not too fragile). If using cedar or a similar leaf, hold it up to the light; it you can't see light through it, snip some of the little branches. Otherwise, the paint will glob in those places. Save compound leaves, such as ash and ferns, for older students because these leaves need to be taken apart and done separately.
2. Gather newspapers and tear them into pieces larger than the leaves. You will need lots of paper, so prepare a good-sized stack beforehand. Also have a sufficient number of wastebaskets handy.
3. Your art specialist, if you have one, may have water-based acrylic paint. Limit color choices to four or less, even for older students. Four 2-ounce bottles should be enough if each student is only printing a couple of leaves. Acrylic paint may be mixed to create different colors. It may be thinned with water if it starts to get too thick. *Do not use poster paint.*
4. Glass beakers are good paint containers because they don't tip over and are easy to wash. Pour the paint into the beakers and set them on desks at a paint station. (If students pour, they have a tendency to empty the whole bottle.)
5. It is a good idea to practice leaf printing before doing it with the class. Buy a remnant or half yard of cotton knit for this purpose. Both sides of the fabric can be used. Interesting patterns can result from this series of tests.
6. Experiment with various thicknesses of paint and with the amount of pressure used when transferring the leaf print to the fabric.

## Procedure
1. Spread each shirt out with room to work. If your room is crowded, consider using lunch tables.
2. Place a large piece of newspaper inside the shirt in case any paint seeps through.
3. Plan the layout. Arrange leaves on the shirt to get an idea of the most appropriate placement and design. Encourage students to choose a simple design.
4. Take one leaf at a time to the paint station. Put a torn piece of newspaper from the stack you prepared on the table or desk. Place the leaf, vein side up, on top of the newspaper. Starting at the petiole, paint toward the outside edges of the leaf. If the leaf is attached to a stem, the stem can be held while painting.
5. Take the paper and painted leaf to the fabric. Carefully lift the leaf from the paper and place paint side down onto the fabric. IMPORTANT: *The paper used to carry the leaf should be immediately thrown into the wastebasket.* Place a clean piece of newspaper over the leaf. Rub and press with your fingers, making sure every part of the leaf comes in contact with the fabric. You should be able to feel the veins and edges through the paper.
6. Check if you have rubbed the leaf enough by lifting one corner of the leaf. It is nearly impossible to place the leaf back into exactly the same position once it has been lifted.
7. Continue this process, one leaf at a time, until the pattern is complete. A favorite leaf can be used again and again. Leaves and colors can also be overlapped to make the design more interesting. (This may not be advisable for younger children.)
8. When the paint is dry to the touch, set the design by placing a dry iron over it for a few seconds. This will assure that the print will not fade when laundered. No pressing cloth is needed.

# Photosynthesis

**Topic**
Photosynthesis

**Key Question**
What is a by-product of photosynthesis?

**Learning Goal**
Students will observe the production of oxygen through photosynthesis.

**Guiding Documents**
*Project 2061 Benchmarks*
- *Some source of "energy" is needed for all organisms to stay alive and grow.*
- *Food provides the fuel and the building material for all organisms. Plants use the energy from light to make sugars from carbon dioxide and water. This food can be used immediately or stored for later use. Organisms that eat plants break down the plant structures to produce the materials and energy they need to survive. Then they are consumed by other organisms.*

*NRC Standards*
- *All organisms cause changes in the environment where they live. Some of these changes are detrimental to the organisms or other organisms, whereas others are beneficial.*
- *For ecosystems, the major source of energy is sunlight. Energy entering ecosystems as sunlight is transferred by producers into chemical energy through photosynthesis. That energy then passes from organism to organism in food webs.*

*NTCM Standard 2000\**
- *Select and apply appropriate standard units and tools to measure length, area, volume, weight, time, temperature, and the size of angles*

**Math**
Measurement
   length

**Science**
Life science
   botany
      photosynthesis

**Integrated Processes**
Observing
Collecting and recording data

**Materials**
*For each group:*
   anacharis (elodea) plant (see *Management*)
   narrow bottle or test tube
   containers for water or clear plastic cups

**Background Information**
    Photosynthesis is a food-making process that occurs in green plants. It is the most important process that goes on in plants. This reaction takes place in the green chloroplasts within the cells of plant leaves and stems. These chloroplasts contain chlorophyll, which absorbs sunlight. Photosynthesis means "putting together with light."

    Carbon dioxide and water in the green chlorophyll of the leaves reacts with sunlight to produce sugar (glucose), oxygen, and water. Molecules of glucose are made up of atoms of carbon, hydrogen, and oxygen. The carbon comes from the carbon dioxide gas in the air.

    The air enters a plant through holes in the leaves called stomata. The oxygen and hydrogen come from water in the soil that enters the plant's roots. The light energy is trapped by a special chemical pigment called chlorophyll. Oxygen, an end product of photosynthesis, is returned to the air.

$$6\,CO_2 + 12\,H_2O \xrightarrow[\text{chlorophyll}]{\text{sunlight}} C_6H_{12}O_6 + 6\,O_2$$

   carbon     water                       glucose  oxygen
   dioxide

    Most photosynthesis takes place in chloroplasts within the cells of plant leaves. (In a cactus, the photosynthesis takes place in the stem.) These chloroplasts contain chlorophyll, which absorbs sunlight. All our food comes from this sunlight-converting activity of green plants. Light energy is converted to chemical energy and is stored in the food made by green plants. Light energy splits the water molecules ($H_2O$) into molecules of hydrogen and oxygen. Hydrogen combines with carbon dioxide to make a simple sugar. The oxygen that is left over from the splitting of the water molecules escapes into the air through stomata.

## Management

1. Anacharis or elodea plants, used in aquariums, can be obtained at a pet store.
2. Divide the class into small groups.

## Procedure

1. Tell students they are going to observe a green plant making its own food, a process called photosynthesis. Give them the observation page.
2. Have each group take a 7- to 8-centimeter piece of elodea and place it, tip first, into a test tube or small bottle filled with water.
3. Instruct students to turn the test tube upside-down in a container half-filled with water and place the container in a bright light.
4. Have students observe, and possibly count, the bubbles of oxygen that escape from the cut end of the elodea. Explain that when the sunlight is absorbed by the green chlorophyll in the leaves and combined with water and carbon dioxide, oxygen is produced as a by-product.
5. Wait 20 minutes, then direct students to measure—in centimeters—the column of oxygen that accumulates at the top of the test tube.
6. Distribute the explanation page and discuss it together. Have students draw a diagram to explain photosynthesis. One suggestion is to start by drawing a plant.

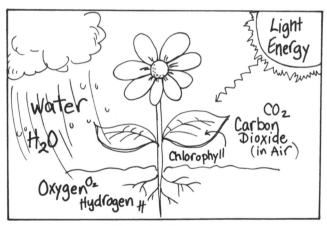

**Sample diagram**

## Connecting Learning

1. What did you observe? [bubbles of oxygen escaping from the elodea]
2. What does a plant need to make food? [light (energy), water (hydrogen and oxygen), and air (carbon dioxide]
3. In what part of a plant does photosynthesis usually take place? [leaves] What in this plant part absorbs light energy? [chloroplasts filled with green chlorophyll]
4. What does photosynthesis produce? [food for the plant (glucose or sugar), oxygen, and water]
5. Why are green plants important to humans? [Green plants add oxygen to the air; they are also a source of food.]
6. In your own words, explain photosynthesis.
7. What, if anything, surprised you about this activity? (Example: the amount of oxygen the plant produced)
8. What are you wondering now?

## Extension

Separate the various pigments in leaves using paper chromatography. You will need a coffee filter, some acetone (available at hardware stores or use fingernail polish remover), a pencil, some tape, a 10-oz clear plastic cup, and non-waxy leaves such as those from a rose bush or bean plant.

*Caution: Acetone can damage finishes, so consider doing this outdoors. If acetone is not allowed in your school, make some samples at home and bring them the next day.*

Cut a coffee filter into strips similar to the pattern shown. Rub or roll a quarter across the leaf at the dotted line of the filter until you have an adequate stain. Attach the filter to a pencil with tape. Pour a small amount of acetone in the cup, just a little more than will cover the bottom. Lay the pencil across the top of the cup so that the pointed part of the filter is in contact with the acetone. Wait for the colors to separate as the acetone moves up the filter. Some leaves only have green pigments.

* Reprinted with permission from *Principles and Standards for School Mathematics, 2000* by the National Council of Teachers of Mathematics. All rights reserved.

# Photosynthesis

## Key Question

What is a by-product of photosynthesis?

 water

## Learning Goal

**Students will:**

- observe the production of oxygen through photosynthesis.

 © 2005 AIMS Education Foundation

# Photosynthesis

## What is a by-product of photosynthesis?

**You will need:**

       7 to 8 cm of an elodea plant
       test tube
       large jar or cut liter bottle
       water

**Do this:**

1. Place a small piece of elodea (water plant) tip first into a test tube of water.

2. Turn the test tube upside-down in a container half-filled with water. Place the container in bright light.

3. Look for bubbles of oxygen. Measure how many centimeters of oxygen collects in 20 minutes.

4. Explain the results of this activity.

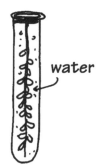

water

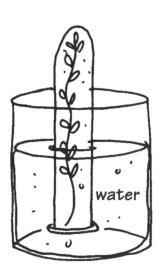

water

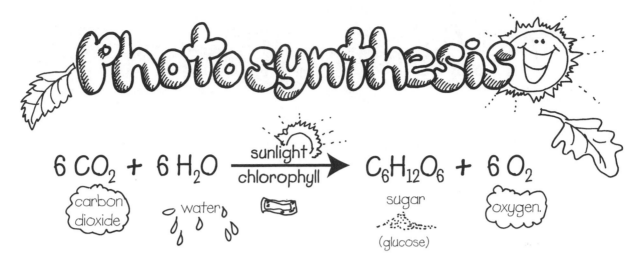

# Photosynthesis

$$6 \, CO_2 + 6 \, H_2O \xrightarrow[\text{chlorophyll}]{\text{sunlight}} C_6H_{12}O_6 + 6 \, O_2$$

carbon dioxide    water    sugar (glucose)    oxygen

Green plants make their own food through a process called photosynthesis. The leaves are the main food-making part of the plant. Leaf cells have chloroplasts with green chlorophyll inside. The chlorophyll absorbs light energy from the sun. Inside the chloroplasts, the plant combines carbon dioxide from the air, hydrogen and oxygen from water in the soil, and light from the sun to make glucose (sugar), water, and oxygen. Plants store this food in leaves, stems, fruits, roots, and seeds. Animals eat plants for energy.

chloroplasts

Draw a diagram to explain photosynthesis.

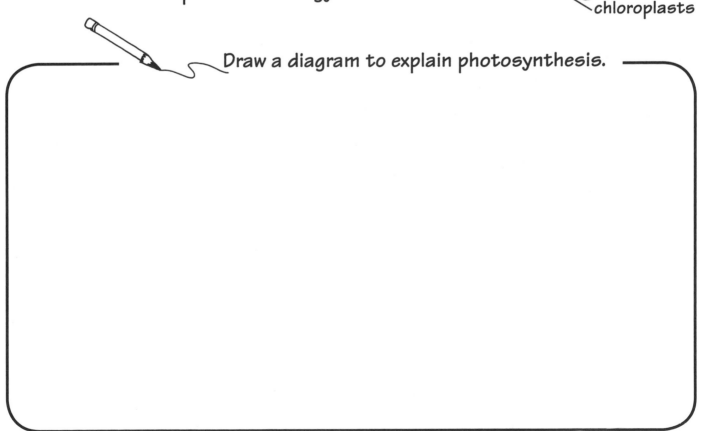

 © 2005 AIMS Education Foundation

# Photosynthesis

1. What did you observe?

2. What does a plant need to make food?

3. In what part of a plant does photosynthesis usually take place? What in this plant part absorbs light energy?

4. What does photosynthesis produce?

5. Why are green plants important to humans?

6. In your own words, explain photosynthesis.

7. What, if anything, surprised you about this activity?

8. What are you wondering now?

# Transpiration

**Topic**
Transpiration of plants

**Key Question**
What happens to the water that plants take in?

**Learning Goal**
Students will observe the transpiration that occurs in plant leaves.

**Guiding Documents**
*Project 2061 Benchmark*
- *Microscopes make it possible to see that living things are made mostly of cells. Some organisms are made of a collection of similar cells that benefit from cooperating. Some organisms' cells vary greatly in appearance and perform very different roles in the organism.*

*NRC Standards*
- *Each plant or animal has different structures that serve different functions in growth, survival, and reproduction. For example, humans have distinct body structures for walking, holding, seeing, and talking.*
- *All organisms cause changes in the environment where they live. Some of these changes are detrimental to the organisms or other organisms, whereas others are beneficial.*

**Science**
Life science
    botany
        transpiration

**Integrated Processes**
Observing
Relating

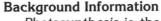

**Materials**
*For each group:*
    indoor or outdoor plant (see *Management 1*)
    hand lens
    clear fingernail polish
    3 or 4 cm of transparent tape
    microscope
    plastic bag
    twist tie or rubber band

**Background Information**
*Photosynthesis* is the main function of a plant's leaves. In order to carry out photosynthesis without the plant dying, the leaves must allow gases such as oxygen, carbon dioxide, and water vapor to enter and leave. This is the role of the thousands of stomata, tiny openings on the underside of each leaf. An open stoma will allow water vapor and gases to pass into and out of the leaf.

*Respiration* is the opposite of photosynthesis. In photosynthesis, energy is used to make sugar (food) and oxygen. In respiration, oxygen is used to break down sugar to produce energy and carbon dioxide. The plant uses the energy to grow, reproduce, and make repairs.

*Transpiration* is the loss of water vapor by evaporation from plant surfaces, mainly through the stomata of the leaves. Water enters the plant through the roots and travels up the plant stems in the xylem tubes to the leaves. Most of the water escapes into the air during transpiration.

**Management**
1. Gather a variety of small plants such as geraniums, ivy, and philodendron, enough so each group can have one. For groups that cannot see the stomata in their fingernail polish samples, have alternate leaves such as ivy, agapanthus (Lily of the Nile), green onion—or even a succulent such as aloe vera—available to make samples; their stomata can be seen under low power.
2. To provide a clean view, use clear rather than frosted tape. Limit fingerprints to the tape's edges.
3. Use plastic bags that do not have a reclosable top.
4. The plants will need bright sunlight or artificial light from a lamp.
5. Set out materials for groups to collect on a table or shelf.

**Procedure**
1. Ask students to recall what they learned in the *Photosynthesis* activity. [A plant, in the process of making food, releases oxygen into the air.]
2. Distribute the activity sheet. Have each group gather a plant and other materials.

3. Tell students to observe the underside of the leaves with a hand lens. Can you see the stomata? [No, they are too small.]
4. Suggest students examine their leaves through a microscope. (They will see green cells, but the stomata will probably be masked by the many layers of cells.)
5. Have students follow the directions for making a leaf sample with fingernail polish. Advise them to coat an area about 1.5 cm long and 0.5 cm wide.
6. Instruct students to observe the sample through a microscope, then draw what they see.

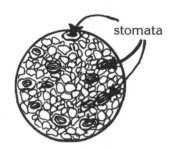
stomata

7. Tell groups to follow the directions for the second investigation at the bottom of the page. Observe the bag every couple of hours until moisture begins to collect. Depending on environmental conditions, it may take from one hour to 48 hours.
8. Once observations have been made, give students the fact page and review it together. Tell them the water in the bag was water that was taken in through the trees roots, but its release into the bag is due to transpiration.
9. On the back of one paper, have students explain what transpiration produced and what happened in the activity. Or student pairs can explain transpiration to each other orally, using evidence from their observations.

## Connecting Learning

1. What is the function of plant leaves? [make food]
2. Pretend your hands are guard cells. Show open and closed stomata.
3. What do the stomata do?
4. What is transpiration? [loss of water through the stomata of leaves]
5. How did the bag show transpiration? [The bag started with leaves and air. After a while, water evaporated from the leaves and condensed as droplets in the bag.]
6. Explain the differences between respiration, photosynthesis, and transpiration.
7. Explain why transpiration and respiration are important to other living things on Earth. [Transpiration is part of the water cycle, adding water vapor to the air and increasing humidity; respiration helps plants grow and reproduce, providing shade, beauty, and food for animals and people.]
8. What are you wondering now?

## Extension

Try the same activity with several variables such as a plant that is very dry, one that is kept in the dark, or another kept at a lower temperature than that of the other plants. Are their stomata open or closed? Do they all release moisture into the bag?

## Curriculum Correlation

*Language Arts*

Write a story as if you were a small bug that had landed on a leaf near a stomata. What would you do? What could you see around you?

# Transpiration

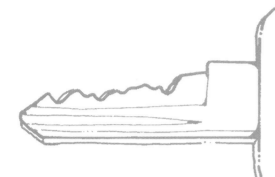

## Key Question

What happens to the water that plants take in?

## Learning Goal

**Students will:**

- observe the transpiration that occurs in plant leaves.

# Transpiration

## You will need:

indoor or outdoor plant
hand lens
clear fingernail polish
3 or 4 cm of transparent tape

microscope
plastic bag
twist tie or rubber band

## What happens to the water produced through photosynthesis?

## Do this:

*Stomata* are tiny openings in leaves that allow gases to enter and leave the plant. Each stoma (single opening) is controlled by two guard cells.

1. Use a hand lens to look for stomata on the underside of a leaf. Can you see them?

2. Look at the underside of the leaf through a microscope. What do you see?

3. Make a leaf sample. Attach a small piece of paper to the tape and label with the plant's name. Paint the underside of the leaf with a heavy coat of fingernail polish. When dry, press the tape over the polish and peel it off the leaf.

4. Observe through a microscope. Draw what you see. ⟶

*microscope view*

## Do this:

1. Place a plastic bag over the green leaves of a plant that is in bright sunlight. Seal the bag with a twist tie or rubber band.

2. After an hour or two, observe the bag. What happens?

3. Remove the bag from the plant.

# Transpiration

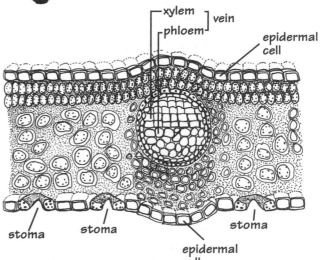

xylem
phloem — vein
epidermal cell
stoma    stoma    stoma
epidermal cell

Tiny openings in leaves, called stomata, allow gases to enter and leave the plant. The stomata take in air that contains the carbon dioxide plants use to make food. Stomata also release most of the oxygen and water. The water changes to water vapor as it evaporates into the air. Depending on air conditions, the water vapor may condense back into water. The evaporation of water from plants, mainly through the stomata, is called *transpiration*. The evaporating water cools the leaves in the same way sweat cools our skin.

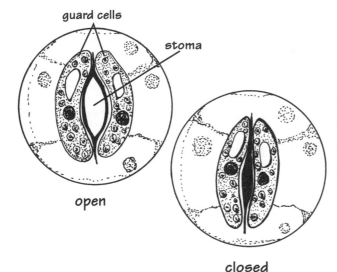

guard cells

stoma

open

closed

Two guard cells control the size of the opening of each stoma (single opening). In sunlight, the guard cells are open so water vapor can escape. At night, they are partly or completely closed so very little water vapor leaves the plant. Other conditions like temperature and humidity also affect whether the guard cells are opened or closed.

## Did you know...

☐ A square centimeter of a leaf may have very few stomata or it may have thousands. It depends on the kind of leaf and environmental conditions.

Transpiration is responsible for about 10 percent of all the water that evaporates into the air.

 © 2005 AIMS Education Foundation

# Transpiration

CONNECTING LEARNING

1. What is the function of plant leaves?

2. Pretend your hands are guard cells. Show open and closed stomata.

3. What do stomata do?

4. What is transpiration?

5. How did the bag show transpiration?

6. Explain the differences between respiration, photosynthesis, and transpiration.

7. Explain why transpiration and respiration are important to other living things on Earth.

8. What are you wondering now?

# Cactus

**Topic**
Cactus

**Key Question**
What features of a cactus help it survive?

**Learning Goals**
Students will:
- observe features of a cactus plant, and
- identify the features a cactus has to help it survive in a desert environment.

**Guiding Documents**
*Project 2061 Benchmarks*
- *Scientific investigations may take many different forms, including observing what things are like or what is happening somewhere, collecting specimens for analysis, and doing experiments. Investigations can focus on physical, biological, and social questions.*
- *For any particular environment, some kinds of plants and animals survive well, some survive less well, and some cannot survive at all.*

*NRC Standards*
- *Each plant or animal has different structures that serve different functions in growth, survival, and reproduction. For example, humans have distinct body structures for walking, holding, seeing, and talking.*
- *Use appropriate tools and techniques to gather, analyze, and interpret data.*

**Science**
Life science
    botany
        plant adaptations

**Integrated Processes**
Observing
Comparing
Collecting and recording data

**Materials**
*For each group:*
    cactus plant (see *Management*)
    hand lens
    knife
    metric ruler

**Background Information**
A cactus is a plant that has adapted to the harsh environment of the desert. The plant has to be able to store the small amount of water it receives during rare rainfalls to use the rest of the year.

The cactus has no leaves to circulate moisture from the roots, so it stores water in its stem. It has a thick, fleshy stem with a waxy covering. The stem holds water and the outside covering keeps the water from evaporating.

Although most cacti have modified their leaves into spines, they carry on the normal food-making activities. The cactus gets energy from sunlight and the stem has taken over the task of making food for the plant.

Cacti have wide-spreading, shallow roots. They spread out a long way around the plant, to collect as much water as possible for storage. Desert plants do not grow close together. Each plant needs to get water and minerals from a large area.

The spines on a cactus protect the plant against damage by animals. The water stored in the stem of a cactus is often the only moisture that an animal can find. Humans use the fruit and pulp of a cactus. The prickly pear bears a sweet, juicy fruit that looks like a pear. The barrel cactus contains a liquid in its stem that can be drunk as water.

**Management**
1. Buy two or three different types of cacti, but enough for each group of four students to have one plant.
2. Caution: Cactus spines can inflict painful punctures. You may want to provide gloves for students to wear while handling the cacti.

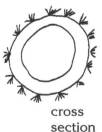

cross section

## Procedure

1. Distribute a cactus to each group of four students.
2. Have students carefully observe the cactus. Invite them to use hand lenses to examine the skin and spines.
3. Instruct students to draw what the cactus looks like on the activity sheet.
4. Direct students to carefully observe one group of spines; spines are modified leaves. Have them draw one on the activity sheet.
5. Have students uproot the cactus plant and examine the roots. Ask them to draw and describe the root system and measure the length of the roots.
6. Tell students to carefully cut the cactus in half horizontally, examine the inside of the cactus, and draw the cross section.
7. Instruct students to describe the inside (pulp) of the cactus. Is the pulp moist? Does it contain water?
8. Have students explain how the adaptations of a cactus help it to live in the desert.

## Connecting Learning

1. How do the inside and outside of a cactus stem compare? [The inside is thick and fleshy; the outside has a waxy covering.]
2. Why do you think the outside is waxy? [The waxy covering helps prevent moisture loss.]
3. How does a cactus stem compare with a herbaceous stem such as a stalk of celery?
4. What part of most cacti are the leaves? [the spines]
5. Where does photosynthesis take place in a cactus? [stem]
6. Is the cactus root system fibrous or taproot? [fibrous]
7. Why is the root system so widespread? [to absorb as much water as possible]
8. What adaptations have cactus plants made? How have they helped the plant survive in the desert? [The waxy covering keeps water from evaporating. The root system spreads over a wide area to absorb as much water as possible. The spines protect the plant from damage by animals.]
9. What are you wondering now?

## Extensions

1. Plant a cactus garden. In a low bowl (or container), put a layer of small pebbles; then spread a thicker layer of planting material over the rocks. Plant specimens of cacti bought from a nursery. Water very lightly. Set the cactus garden in the window where it will get six hours of direct sunlight.
2. To compare the water that evaporates from a cactus and the water that evaporates from a green leafy plant of similar size, place a plastic bag over a cactus and another bag over the leafy plant. Set each in the sunlight for a day. Compare the moisture content in the plastic bags.

## Curriculum Correlation

*Social Studies*

Research how widespread the area is where cacti grow naturally. Find out how many cacti provide products for humans.

# Cactus

## Key Question

What features of a cactus help it survive?

## Learning Goals

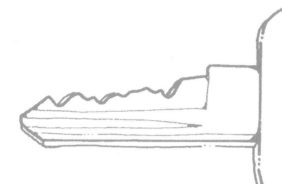

Students will:

- observe features of a cactus plant, and

- identify the features a cactus has to help it survive in a desert environment.

# Cactus

## Adaptation Study

1.  Observe a cactus plant. Draw and describe in detail.

Measure
    height: _____ circumference: _____

2.  Uproot the plant and draw the root system. Describe:

Measure length of roots: _____

3.  Cut the cactus in half. Draw the cross section.

Cactus

Spine

Roots

4.  How do the adaptations of a cactus help it live in the desert?

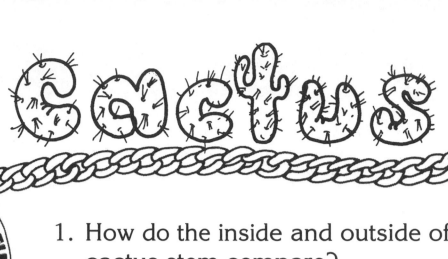

# Cactus

CONNECTING LEARNING

1. How do the inside and outside of a cactus stem compare?

2. Why do you think the outside is waxy?

3. How does a cactus stem compare with a herbaceous stem such as a stalk of celery?

4. What part of most cacti are the leaves?

5. Where does photosynthesis take place in a cactus?

6. Is the cactus root system fibrous or taproot?

7. Why is the root system so widespread?

8. What adaptations have cactus plants made? How have they helped the plant survive in the desert?

9. What are you wondering now?

# New Plant Discovery!

## Topic
Plant adaptations

## Challenge
Design a plant with special adaptations for a chosen environment.

## Learning Goal
Students will design and make a plant that is adapted to a certain type of environment.

## Guiding Documents
*Project 2061 Benchmark*
- *For any particular environment, some kinds of plants and animals survive well, some survive less well, and some cannot survive at all.*
- *Some source of "energy" is needed for all organisms to stay alive and grow.*

*NRC Standards*
- *Each plant or animal has different structures that serve different functions in growth, survival, and reproduction. For example, humans have distinct body structures for walking, holding, seeing, and talking.*
- *An organism's patterns of behavior are related to the nature of that organism's environment, including the kinds and numbers of other organisms present, the availability of food and resources, and the physical characteristics of the environment. When the environment changes, some plants and animals survive and reproduce, and others die or move to new locations.*

## Science
Life science
    botany
        plant adaptations

## Integrated Processes
Observing
Relating

## Materials
Scraps of materials such as:
| | |
|---|---|
| construction paper | yarn |
| aluminum foil | crayons |
| cloth scraps | twigs |
| string | clay |
| toothpicks | leaves |
| chenille stems | |

## Background Information
Most regions support a wide variety of plants. Gardens, parks, city streets, vacant lots, forests, grasslands, deserts, and aquatic locations all have their own assortment of plants. Each species of plants displays a unique combination of characteristics that enables it to survive under specific environmental conditions such as amount of wind, water, light, and temperature.

Adaptations are features of organisms that help them to survive and reproduce. Examples of plant adaptations include the following: the water-storing cells in the barrel cactus; the sharp, protective spines on the thistle; the fire-resistant bark of the redwood tree; runner stems of strawberry plants; and banyan trees with roots from branches for support. Some plants have leaves to trap insects. Grape vines have stem tendrils to help them climb. Cacti have fibrous roots that are shallow and branch widely. Corn has prop roots to help hold it up.

## Management
1. Discuss what students will be making several days prior to the activity so they can bring additional materials to make their own plants.
2. Put limits on the size of the creation.
3. To give students some ideas, copy the *Insect-eat-um-up-us* (next page) on a transparency.
4. This can be used as a culminating activity or as a performance assessment for a plant unit.

## Procedure
1. Discuss plant adaptations. Have students generate a list on the board or chart paper.
2. Tell students that they are going to invent and build a particular type of plant with special adaptations for its environment. Encourage them to be creative. For example, they might make a plant that can withstand smog (gas mask) or acid rain (umbrella); they might make a plant that can grow with low moisture (modified stem or leaves).

students started, offer some suggestions
a plant that:

apons for self-defense

re water

nimals that feed on it

ive when grazed on by cattle and sheep

hen periodically covered with salt water

- can survive high winds
- can live even if it is burned by fire
- a cow won't eat
- can live without being watered
- will drown insects that try to eat it
- can live at the edge of a glacier
- can grow in a crack in a concrete sidewalk

4. Give students the activity sheet. Have them record their new inventions by drawing a picture, labeling the special features, and naming the new species.
5. Ask students to describe the plant's environment and physical features on the sheet.

## Connecting Learning

1. In what kind of environment does your plant live?
2. What features help your plant adapt to its environment?
3. Did anyone else design a plant for this same environment? If so, how is your plant alike or different?
4. What are you wondering now?

## Curriculum Correlation

*Literacy*

Have students use their notes from the activity page to write a newspaper article or an article for a scientific journal.

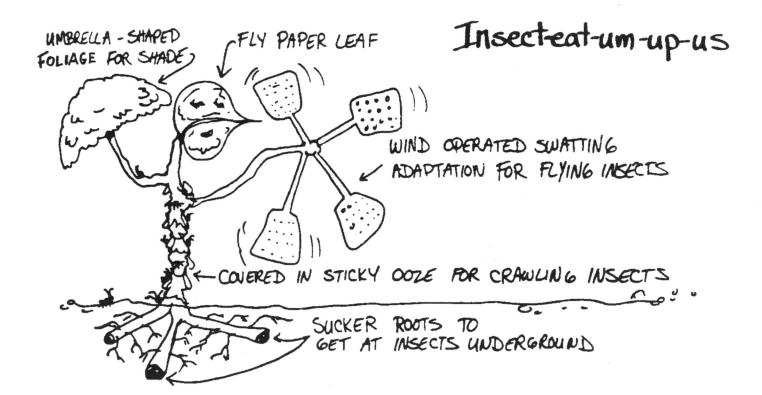

UMBRELLA-SHAPED FOLIAGE FOR SHADE

FLY PAPER LEAF

Insect-eat-um-up-us

WIND OPERATED SWATTING ADAPTATION FOR FLYING INSECTS

COVERED IN STICKY OOZE FOR CRAWLING INSECTS

SUCKER ROOTS TO GET AT INSECTS UNDERGROUND

© 2005 AIMS Education Foundation

# New Plant Discovery!

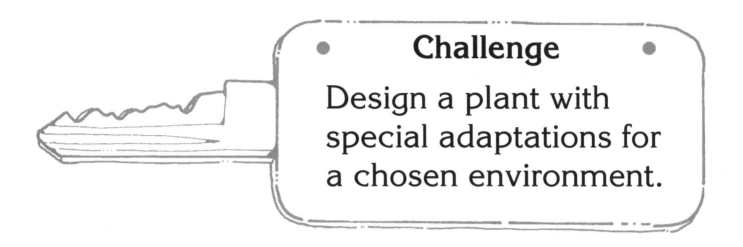

## Challenge

Design a plant with special adaptations for a chosen environment.

## Learning Goal

**Students will:**

* design and make a plant that is adapted to a certain type of environment.

# New Plant Discovery!

**Who** is the discoverer?

**What** is the name of plant?

**When** did the discovery occur?

**Where** did the discovery occur?

## Exclusive Photo

_____

_____

_caption_

## DESCRIPTIONS • Adaptations

Environment: _____

_____

_____

_____

Leaves: _____

_____

_____

_____

Stem: _____

_____

_____

_____

Roots: _____

_____

_____

_____

Flowers/Seeds: _____

_____

_____

# New Plant Discovery!

CONNECTING LEARNING

1. In what kind of environment does your plant live?

2. What features help your plant adapt to its environment?

3. Did anyone else design a plant for this same environment? If so, how is your plant alike or different?

4. What are you wondering now?

                © 2005 AIMS Education Foundation

# Cell Facts

The cell is the basic unit of life. All living things are made up of one or more cells, but most are so small that they are visible only under a microscope. There are hundreds of cells in a single leaf on a tree.

The living cell has three main parts: the cell membrane, the cytoplasm, and the nucleus. The *cell membrane* is a very thin structure that regulates what substances enter and leave the cell. The *cytoplasm* is the jelly-like substance—containing water, salts, and organic compounds—that fills the cell. Suspended in the cytoplasm is the *nucleus,* the round structure that controls the cell's functions.

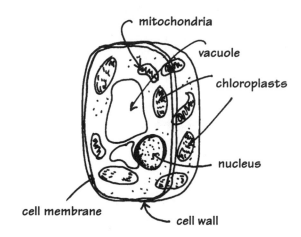

In plants, a thick *cell wall* encloses each cell, giving the cell a defined rectangular shape. The cell wall in most plants contains cellulose. This is what gives the cell strength; it also protects the delicate cell contents.

A closer look reveals a variety of tiny structures or *organelles* suspended in the cytoplasm. The differently-shaped organelles—spheres, discs, rods—each performs a specific job that contributes to the life of the cell. They take in nutrients, convert nutrients into energy, store and release energy, get rid of wastes, grow, and reproduce. Thousands upon thousands of chemical reactions are carried out every minute inside of the cell.

Among the larger organelles are *vacuoles,* some of which look like tiny air bubbles. These cell parts store food and water in a watery fluid called cell sap until the cell is ready to use them. Some vacuoles also store wastes until the cell is ready to get rid of them.

Another type of organelle is the sausage-shaped *mitochondria.* These power stations burn fuel (sugar), producing most of the energy the cell needs to live and function, and leave behind water and carbon dioxide as waste products. Mitochondria are extremely minute and cannot be seen with a low-power microscope.

The cytoplasm of plant cells may also have small oval-shaped *chloroplasts.* They contain several pigments including the green chlorophylls, yellow xanthophylls, and red or orange carotenoids. Using the energy of sunlight, the chloroplasts produce sugar by photosynthesis. All life on Earth depends on these plant sugars.

*Ribosomes* (protein factories) and *endoplasmic reticulum* (transport membranes) are other organelles located in the cytoplasm.

Cell tissues are masses of similar cells working together to perform a special job. Plants have many specialized tissues—growth tissues, food-making tissues, strength and support tissues, and protective tissues. A group of tissues, bringing together a variety of jobs, is called a tissue system. For example, the xylem and phloem are part of the vascular tissue system. Both are conducting tissue, but each serves a different function. Tissue systems form organs that work together to carry on the life functions for the plant.

One of the most important features of a cell is its ability to divide itself into two identical cells, a process called *mitosis.* All cells come from other cells. This is the way organisms grow and replace worn or damaged parts. Lower plant life, such as algae, mosses, and ferns, rely on mitosis to produce spores.

                    © 2005 AIMS Education Foundation

# Model of a CELL

## Topic
Plant cells

## Key Question
How does your model represent a plant cell?

## Learning Goals
Students will:
- learn about the structure and function of a plant cell, and
- build a cell model.

## Guiding Documents

*Project 2061 Benchmarks*
- *All living things are composed of cells, from just one to many millions, whose details usually are visible only through a microscope. Different body tissues and organs are made up of different kinds of cells. The cells in similar tissues and organs in other animals are similar to those in human beings but differ somewhat from cells found in plants.*
- *Within cells, many of the basic functions of organisms—such as extracting energy from food and getting rid of waste—are carried out. The way in which cells function is similar in all living organisms.*

*NRC Standards*
- *All organisms are composed of cells—the fundamental unit of life. Most organisms are single cells; other organisms, including humans, are multicellular.*
- *Cells carry on the many functions needed to sustain life. They grow and divide, thereby producing more cells. This requires that they take in nutrients, which they use to provide energy for the work that cells do and to make the materials that a cell or an organism needs.*

## Science
Life science
    botany
        plant cells

## Integrated Processes
Observing
Comparing and contrasting
Relating

## Materials

*For each group:*
    small reclosable plastic bag
    table tennis ball or small water balloon
    small handful of pinto or small kidney beans
    small handful unshelled peanuts
    small handful birdseed
    water
    tray

*For the classroom:*
    overhead projector and transparency

## Background Information (See *Cell Facts.*)

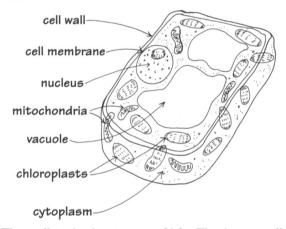

The cell is the basic unit of life. The living cell has three main parts: the cell membrane, the cytoplasm, and the nucleus. The cell membrane is a very thin, important structure that regulates what substances enter and leave the cell cytoplasm. Inside the cell is the cytoplasm; it contains organelles that have different jobs. Energy for the cell is produced in minute sausage-shaped power stations called mitochondria. Mitochondria are numerous, but so tiny they are difficult to see, even with a powerful microscope. Ribosomes (protein factories), chloroplasts, and endoplasmic reticulum (transport membranes) are other organelles.

Also located in the cytoplasm are the vacuoles. These tiny structures store food and water in a fluid until the cell is ready to use them. Some vacuoles also store wastes.

The nucleus is where the cell's information is stored. Here, all the instructions that the cell needs to live and work are housed.

In plants, a thick cell wall encloses each cell. This is what gives the cell strength and support and protects the delicate cell contents.

## Management

1. Lay out materials for groups to gather: the reclosable plastic bag for the cell membrane, the table tennis ball or small water balloon for the nucleus, the unshelled peanuts for the larger organelles, and the beans and birdseed for the smaller bodies in the cytoplasm.
2. Make a transparency of the *Plant Cell* sheet.

## Procedure

1. Use the *Plant Cell* fact sheet to introduce the names and functions of the various structures of a cell.
2. Suggest students relate the structure and functions of the cell to a factory:

   factory walls and doors ⟷ cell membrane
   power plant ⟷ mitochondria
   main office ⟷ nucleus

3. Distribute the *Make a Model of a Cell* sheet. Have groups gather materials, make plans, and construct their cell models. [Place the ball or balloon in the bag to represent the nucleus in the cell membrane. Drop in peanuts or paper clips to represent larger bodies in the cytoplasm, and a small handful of beans or birdseed to represent the smaller bodies in the cytoplasm.]
4. Instruct students to draw and label their cell models.
5. To give students an idea of what a cell would look like under a microscope, put a completed cell model on the overhead projector.
6. To show students what a group of cells would look like under a microscope, collect all of the cell models in a clear container.

## Connecting Learning

1. How is your model like a plant cell? [The bag represents the cell membrane, the ball represents the nucleus, etc.]
2. How is it different? [It isn't filled with liquid. It doesn't have a cell wall.]
3. How could we represent a cell wall? [Make a "collar" out of card stock to go around the plastic bag.]
4. How are the parts of a factory like the parts of a cell?
5. Why are the mitochondria important? [releases stored energy (respiration) so the plant can grow, reproduce, and make repairs]
6. What is the purpose of the cell membrane? How is it similar to factory walls?
7. What happens in the chloroplasts? [photosynthesis—chlorophyll takes sunlight, carbon dioxide, and water to make food (glucose or sugar)]
8. What are you wondering now?

## Extensions

1. Use the *Cell Cookies* recipe to make a different model of a cell.
2. Have students use scrap materials to glue together a two-dimensional model of a cell on construction paper.
3. Suggest students role-play the parts of a cell.

          © 2005 AIMS Education Foundation

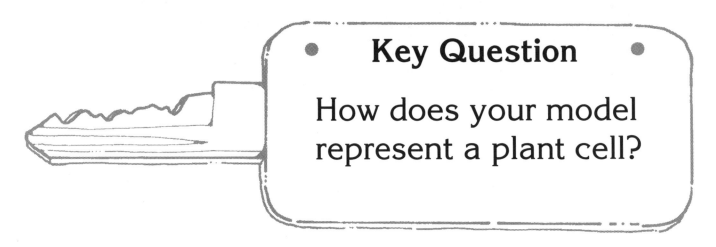

## Key Question

How does your model represent a plant cell?

## Learning Goals

**Students will:**

- learn about the structure and function of a plant cell, and

- build a cell model.

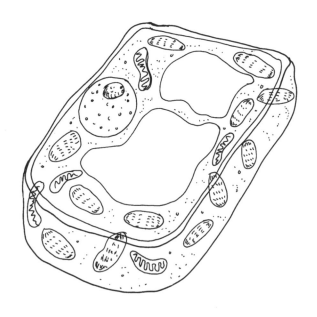

# Plant Cell

# Model of a Cell

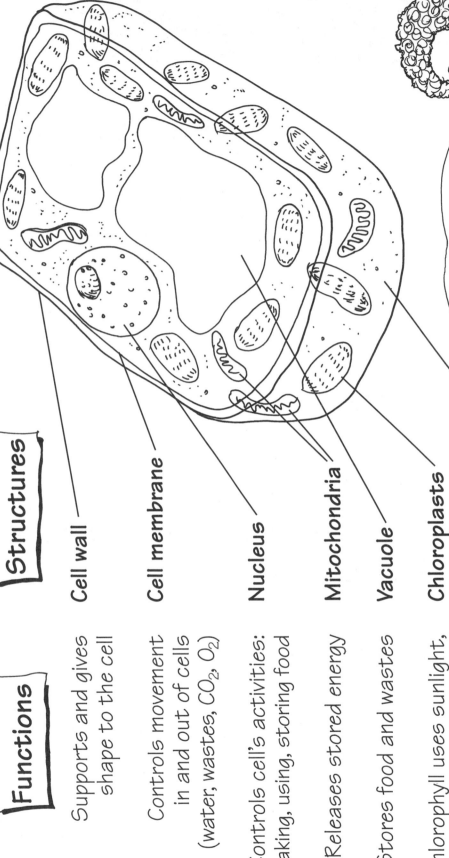

Work with a group to make a mental model. Compare a plant cell to your classroom. Share your model with the class.

## Structures

Cell wall

Cell membrane

Nucleus

Mitochondria

Vacuole

Chloroplasts

Cytoplasm

## Functions

Supports and gives shape to the cell

Controls movement in and out of cells (water, wastes, $CO_2$, $O_2$)

Controls cell's activities: making, using, storing food

Releases stored energy

Stores food and wastes

Chlorophyll uses sunlight, $CO_2$, and water to make food (sugar)

Contains cell's materials

# Make a Model of a CELL

## You will need:

Reclosable plastic bag
Water
Tray
Objects to represent organelles:

small beans
peanuts    bird seed

ball or water balloon

## Do this:

1. Study the diagram of a plant cell.
   Think about the function of each structure.

2. Plan a three-dimensional model.
   How will you represent each structure?

Chloroplasts: _____
Mitochondria: _____
Cell wall: _____
Nucleus: _____
Vacuoles: _____
Cytoplasm: _____

3. Make your model. Draw a diagram and label each structure.

# Model of a CELL

## Cell Cookies

*Measure carefully.*

1 cup margarine (soft)
3/4 cup white sugar
3/4 cup light brown sugar
1 teaspoon vanilla

2 eggs
2 1/4 cups unsifted flour
1 teaspoon baking soda
1/2 teaspoon salt

Extras: round candies, other candies, raisins, dates, nuts, fruits, peanuts, chocolate chips, sprinkles

\* Makes 3-4 dozen

1. Cream margarine, sugar, brown sugar, and vanilla until light and fluffy. Add eggs and beat well.

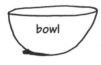     

2. Combine flour, baking soda, and salt. Gradually beat into the creamed mixture.

3. Mold the dough into the shape of a cell. Build the model with the extras.

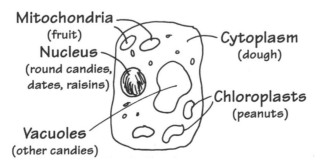

Mitochondria (fruit)
Nucleus (round candies, dates, raisins)
Cytoplasm (dough)
Chloroplasts (peanuts)
Vacuoles (other candies)

4. Bake on an ungreased cookie sheet at 375° for 8 to 10 minutes. Cool slightly, remove, and

## Enjoy!

# Model of a CELL

**CONNECTING LEARNING**

1. How is your model like a plant cell?

2. How is it different?

3. How could we represent a cell wall?

4. How are the parts of a factory like the parts of a cell?

5. Why are the mitochondria important?

6. What is the purpose of the cell membrane? How is it similar to factory walls?

7. What happens in the chloroplasts?

8. What are you wondering now?

# Focus on Cells

## Topic
Plant cell structures

## Key Question
What do you observe about onion cells under a microscope?

## Learning Goals
Students will:
- learn how to make a wet mount slide, and
- make observations about the structure of onion cells.

## Guiding Documents
*Project 2061 Benchmarks*
- *Microscopes make it possible to see that living things are made mostly of cells. Some organisms are made of a collection of similar cells that benefit from cooperating. Some organisms' cells vary greatly in appearance and perform very different roles in the organism.*
- *Within cells, many of the basic functions of organisms—such as extracting energy from food and getting rid of waste—are carried out. The way in which cells function is similar in all living organisms.*

*NRC Standards*
- *All organisms are composed of cells—the fundamental unit of life. Most organisms are single cells; other organisms, including humans, are multicellular.*
- *Cells carry on the many functions needed to sustain life. They grow and divide, thereby producing more cells. This requires that they take in nutrients, which they use to provide energy for the work that cells do and to make the materials that a cell or an organism needs.*

## Math
Geometric shapes
Estimation

## Science
Life science
botany
cell structure

## Integrated Processes
Observing
Collecting and recording data
Comparing and contrasting
Relating

## Materials
*For the class:*
whole white onion (see *Management 1*)
overhead transparency of *Plant Cell Structures*

*For each group:*
microscope
microscope slide
cover slip
tweezers
methylene blue (see *Management 3*))
eyedropper or pipette
water
newspapers

## Background Information
The body of most plants is made up of roots, stems, and leaves—all of which are composed of cells. The life activities of a plant take place within the cell. Cells have special structures that perform these activities.

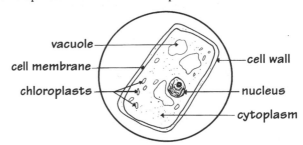

The *nucleus* is the most prominent feature of the cell. It is the control center, regulating all the processes that occur within the cell. Other important plant cell structures are the *cell wall* which provides support and protection, the *cell membrane* which allows dissolved material to enter and leave the cell, the *vacuoles* which store food and waste, the *chloroplasts* which contain the green chlorophyll used to make food, and *cytoplasm* in which the organelles are suspended.

Plant cells differ from animal cells in that they have cell walls. Plant cells may have chloroplasts, but most animal cells don't. The cells in underground parts of plants, such as onion bulbs, are not exposed to light so they do not develop chloroplasts. The green chlorophyll in chloroplasts needs light energy to make food.

What you will be able to see in either a wet mount or a stained wet mount onion skin slide will depend upon the magnifying power of your microscope and the quality of the wet mount slides. The basic cell shape should be visible at even 20X, the nucleus at 50X or higher.

## Management

1. If you want students to learn how to prepare stained wet mount slides, use white onions. Otherwise, red onion skins have enough contrast so stain is not needed.
2. To make it easier to separate the onion's membrane, cut the onion in half and soak in half-filled cups of water overnight.
3. Have tweezers, eyedroppers or pipettes, water, and methylene blue ready. Methylene blue is available from AIMS. Pipettes release a smaller amount of fluid than eyedroppers.
4. Have students stain their slides at special stations located around the room. Put bottles of stain in tip-proof boxes and set these boxes on newspaper. Caution: Methylene blue stains skin and clothing.
5. This activity will take about two 45-minute periods.

## Procedure

### Wet Mount Slide

1. Use the overhead transparency of *Plant Cell Structures* to inform students about what they are going to observe.
2. Distribute the *Wet Mount Slide* sheet and review the directions for making a wet mount slide. Have students clean the slide and cover slip.
3. Direct students to break an onion slice in two and carefully pull the slice apart.
4. Instruct students to use tweezers to pull off a very thin piece of onion skin or membrane.
5. Have students place the skin in the center of the slide, spreading and flattening it to eliminate folds. A small drop of water under the skin may be helpful.
6. Tell students to add a drop of water to the onion skin, place a cover slip over it, and carefully press down to remove any air bubbles.
7. Direct students to place the slide on the stage of the microscope, set it to low power, and adjust until the cells are in focus. Ask them to draw a few cells—just as they appear through the lens—and label the cell wall.
8. Have students switch to high power, then draw and label what they see.

### Staining Cells

1. If doing staining on the same day, have students use their wet mount slides from the first part of the activity. Otherwise, have students prepare new wet mount slides.
2. Give students the *Staining Cells* sheet and read through the directions together.
3. Tell students to lift up the cover slip and add a drop of methylene blue to the slide. Methylene blue makes the cell wall and nucleus darker than the rest of the cell, so the structures are more noticeable.

4. Instruct students to lower the cover slip and examine the cells on low power, then on high power.
5. Have students draw what they see and label the structures they can see under high power (cell wall, nucleus, cytoplasm, though probably not the cell membrane).
6. Distribute the *Plant Cell Structures/Functions* sheet. Direct students to label structures and describe functions, drawing from prior knowledge (see *Model of a Cell*). Give guidance where needed.
7. Invite students to give evidence that onion skin cells do or do not have chloroplasts and discuss the reason why.

## Connecting Learning

1. What is the general shape of the onion skin cells? [rectangular]
2. Estimate the number of onion cells you can see under high power. What does this tell you about onion skin? [There are a lot of cells, even in a little piece of onion skin.]
3. Why do you think there are many cells close together? [The rectangular cells press against each other without any gaps, providing strength and protection.]
4. Why did we use stain to observe the onion cells? [The stain makes some parts of the cell darker than other parts so you can better identify them.]
5. What cell structures are visible? [the cell wall, nucleus, and cytoplasm] Is a line on the inside of the cell walls visible? (The cell membrane is probably not visible.)
6. All plant cells have cell walls. What is the function of the cell wall? [provide strength and protection]
7. What is the control center of the cell? [the nucleus] Where is it located? [in the cytoplasm]
8. How do you know if onion skin cells have chloroplasts? [The chlorophyll in chloroplasts gives leaves and other plant parts their green color. Onion skin is not green.] Why do you think this is? [Onion bulbs grow underground where there is no light, so there is no need for chloroplasts. Chloroplasts need light to make food.]
9. What are you wondering now?

## Extension

Compare the skin cells of other fruits and vegetables with that of the onion skin.

## Curriculum Correlation

Research the history of the microscope and its importance to science.

# Focus on Cells

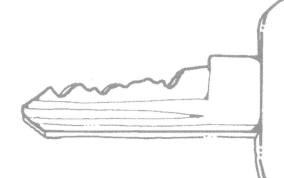

## Key Question

What do you observe about onion cells under a microscope?

## Learning Goals

### Students will:

- learn how to make a wet mount slide, and

- make observations about the structure of onion cells.

 © 2005 AIMS Education Foundation

# Focus on Cells

## Plant Cell Structures

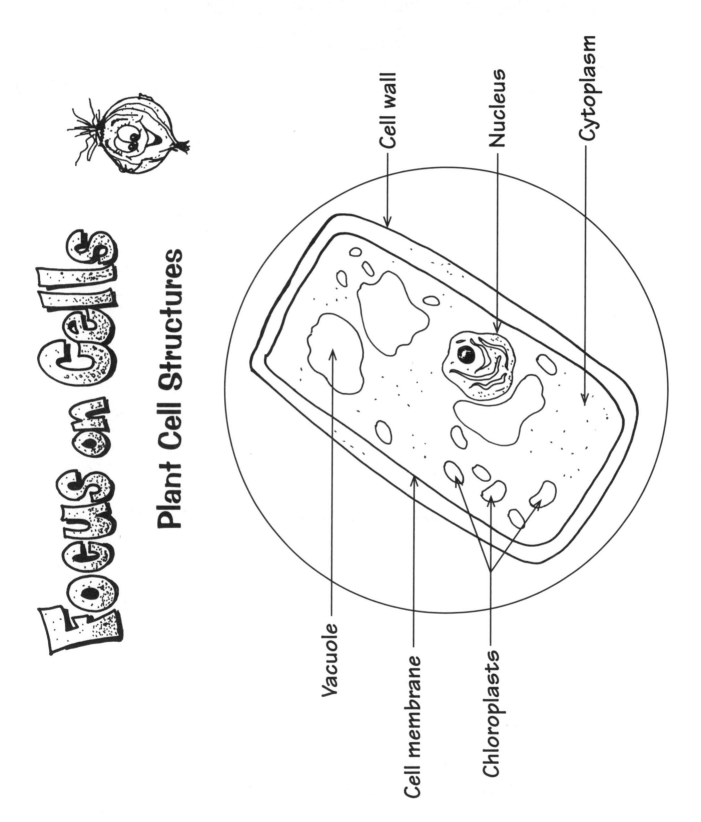

Cell wall

Nucleus

Cytoplasm

Vacuole

Cell membrane

Chloroplasts

© 2005 AIMS Education Foundation

# Focus on Cells

## Wet Mount Slide

1. Pull the onion slice apart.

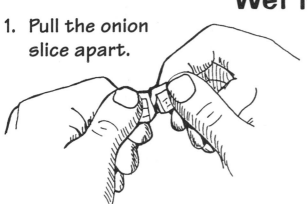

2. Pull off a thin piece of skin.

3. Place the onion skin on the center of the slide. Add a drop of water and then the cover slip. Place on the microscope stage.

4. Observe the onion skin under low power. Draw a few cells and label the cell wall.

Low Power

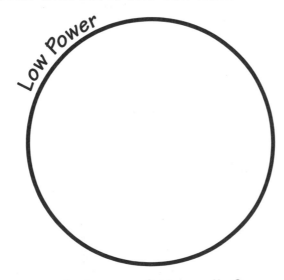

What is the general shape of the cells?

5. Switch to high power.

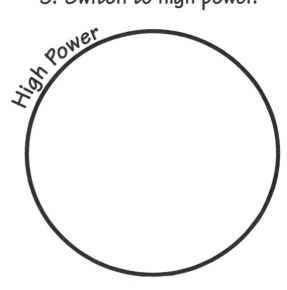

High Power

# Focus on Cells

## Staining Cells

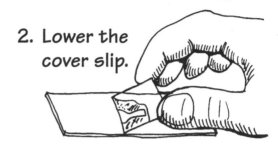

1. Lift the cover slip. Add a drop of methylene blue.

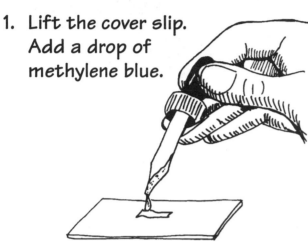

2. Lower the cover slip.

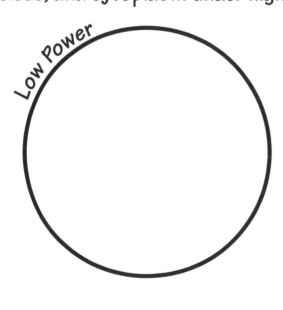

3. Why did you add stain to the cells?

4. Draw the cells under low power. Draw the cells and label the cell wall, nucleus, and cytoplasm under high power.

Low Power

High Power

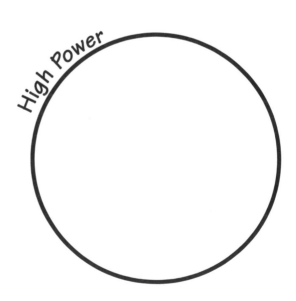

Estimate the number of onion cells you can see under high power. _____
What does this tell you about onion skin?

# Plant Cell Structures

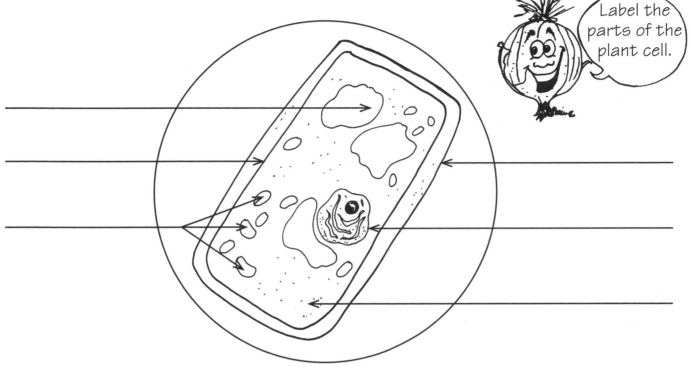

Label the parts of the plant cell.

## Plant Cell Functions

Cell wall: _____

Cell membrane: _____

Nucleus: _____

Cytoplasm: _____

Vacuole: _____

Chloroplasts: _____

Onions are plants. Plant cells may have chloroplasts.
How do you know if onion skin cells have chloroplasts?
Why do you think this is?

# Focus on Cells

CONNECTING LEARNING

1. What is the general shape of the onion skin cells?

2. Estimate the number of onion cells you can see under high power. What does this tell you about onion skin?

3. Why do you think there are many cells close together?

4. Why did we use stain to observe the onion cells?

5. What cell structures are visible? Is a line on the inside of the cell walls visible?

6. All plant cells have cell walls. What is the function of the cell wall?

7. What is the control center of the cell? Where is it located?

8. How do you know if onion skin cells have chloroplasts? Why do you think this is?

9. What are you wondering now?

# Cell Your Fruits and Vegetables

## Topic
Plant cells

## Key Question
How do the cells of various fruits and vegetables compare?

## Learning Goal
Students will compare the cells of various fruits and vegetables.

## Guiding Documents
*Project 2061 Benchmark*
- *Microscopes make it possible to see that living things are made mostly of cells. Some organisms are made of a collection of similar cells that benefit from cooperating. Some organisms' cells vary greatly in appearance and perform very different roles in the organism.*

*NRC Standard*
- *All organisms are composed of cells—the fundamental unit of life. Most organisms are single cells; other organisms, including humans, are multicellular.*

## Science
Life science
    botany
        cell structure

## Integrated Processes
Observing
Collecting and recording data
Comparing and contrasting
Relating

## Materials
*For the class:*
    variety of fruits and vegetables (see *Management 1*)
    potato peeler or razor blade (see *Management 2*)

*For each group:*
    microscope
    4 microscope slides
    4 cover slips
    tweezers
    methylene blue (see *Management 4*)
    eyedropper or pipette
    water
    paper towels
    newspapers

## Background Information
Though all cells have many similarities, they also have many differences. They differ in size, shape, texture, color, and other attributes. Tissues from two fruits, such as an apple and a pear, may appear to be similar at first glance, but microscopic examination can reveal contrasts between them.

A tissue is a group of similar cells performing the same job. A group of tissues, bringing together a variety of jobs, is called a tissue system. There are three basic categories of plant tissue systems: dermal or protective tissue (epidermis); ground tissue (like the fleshy part of fruit) providing food storage, support, and/or photosynthesis; and vascular or conducting tissue (xylem and phloem). In this case, we will be observing the skin or dermal tissue of fruits and vegetables.

## Management
1. Beforehand, collect a variety of fruits and vegetables such as garlic, lettuce, celery, oranges, pears, and grapes. Any red grape skin shows cells well.
2. Prepare tissue samples using a potato peeler or razor blade (adults only). Slice a thin piece of skin from grapes, carrots, pears, etc. Take membrane samples from the inside curve of onions and celery. Use the membrane covering an orange or lemon section.
3. Have materials ready for groups to collect.
4. Set up special stations for student to stain their slides. Methylene blue is available from AIMS. Put bottles of methylene blue in tip-proof boxes and set these boxes on newspaper. Caution: Methylene blue stains skin and clothing.
5. See the *Focus on Cells* activity for instructions on preparing wet mount slides.
6. Do not taste any of the food tissue used in this investigation.

## Procedure

1. Ask students to share what they know about cells. Present the *Key Question,* "How do the cells of various fruits and vegetables compare?"

2. Explain that a tissue is a group of similar cells performing the same job. They will be comparing a group of tissues, called a tissue system, which forms the skin of fruits and vegetables. Its job is to protect.

3. Review the procedure for making a stained wet mount slide—put a thin piece of tissue on a slide, add a drop of water and a drop of methylene blue, put a cover slip over it, and view through the microscope.

4. Distribute the activity sheet and instruct groups to collect materials.

5. Have each group prepare four wet mount slides of different fruit and vegetable tissues.

6. Direct students to make and record observations on the sheet.

7. After sufficient time, instruct students to clean up and collect the materials.

8. Have the students in each group compare notes, then write a summary of their findings.

## Connecting Learning

1. How were your tissue samples similar? [generally rectangular shape]

2. How were your tissue samples different? [size of cells, for one]

3. Which fruit or vegetable was the easiest to observe? Why? [greater color contrast, larger cells, etc.]

4. Which tissue has cells that are most nearly square?

5. What other observations did you make?

6. We took tissue from the skin of fruits and vegetables. What is the job of skin? [to protect the fruit or vegetable]

7. What are you wondering now?

## Extension

The cytoplasm in cells is mostly water. Dry some fruits and vegetables and examine the tissue through a microscope. How do the cells of a dried apple compare with those of a fresh apple? (or any other fruit or vegetable)

## Curriculum Correlation

*Social Studies*

Have students research and make a list of the fruits and vegetables that are grown in their county.

# CELL Your Fruits and Vegetables

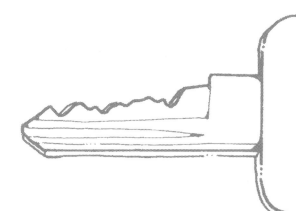

## Key Question

How do the cells of various fruits and vegetables compare?

## Learning Goal

*Students will:*

- compare the cells of various fruits and vegetables.

 Your **Fruits** and **Vegetables**

## How do cells of fruits and vegetables compare?

Choose four types of fruits or vegetables. Carefully pull plant tissue from each one and make wet mount slides. Observe with a microscope.

### Draw:                                                    ### Describe:

**Slide # 1**

Name: _____

Tissue location: _____

Color: _____

Cell shape: _____

Other: _____

_____

**Slide # 2**

Name: _____

Tissue location: _____

Color: _____

Cell shape: _____

Other: _____

_____

**Slide # 3**

Name: _____

Tissue location: _____

Color: _____

Cell shape: _____

Other: _____

_____

**Slide # 4**

Name: _____

Tissue location: _____

Color: _____

Cell shape: _____

Other: _____

_____

Use your notes to write a summary of your findings.

# CELL Your Fruits and Vegetables

1. How were your tissue samples similar?

2. How were your tissue samples different?

3. Which fruit or vegetable was the easiest to observe? Why?

4. Which tissue has cells that are most nearly square?

5. What other observations did you make?

6. We took tissue from the skin of fruits and vegetables. What is the job of skin?

7. What are you wondering now?

 © 2005 AIMS Education Foundation

# Glossary

**adaptation**   a change in the structure and form of a plant to fit different conditions

**angiosperm**   a flowering plant that produces seed within fruits

**anther**   the part of the stamen of a flower that bears the pollen

**axil**   the angle formed between a twig and the petiole of a leaf

**cambium**   the growth tissue of plant stems that produces new xylem and phloem cells

**carotenoid**   a group of orange to red pigments found in various plant tissues

**calyx**   all the sepals of a flower

**cell membrane**   the outer boundary of the cell that determines what enters and leaves the cell

**cell wall**   the rigid cellulose protective layer that surrounds the plant cell

**chlorophyll**   the green pigment that allows green plants to use sunlight to make food

**chloroplasts**   the plant cell part that contains the green pigment chlorophyll

**conifer**   a tree or shrub with needlelike leaves that produces seeds in cones

**corolla**   all the petals of a flower

**cotyledon**   a seed leaf that usually stores food

**cytoplasm**   a jelly-like material surrounding the nucleus in a cell

**dicotyledon**   (dicot) a group of flowering plants that have seeds with two seed leaves

**dispersal**   the process of the spreading of seeds from the parent plant to another area

**dormant**   a period of inactivity and resting in seeds, buds, and plants

**embryo**   the tiny plant within a seed

| | |
|---|---|
| **endosperm** | stored food in the seeds |
| **epicotyl** | the part of the stem that is above the cotyledons in the embryo of a plant |
| **fertilization** | the joining of the sperm cell with the egg cell |
| **fibrous root** | branching, threadlike roots |
| **filament** | the stalklike part of a stamen that supports the anther |
| **germinate** | to begin to grow or sprout |
| **glucose** | a kind of simple sugar |
| **gymnosperm** | a plant whose seeds are produced in cones |
| **internode** | a stem region between nodes |
| **lignin** | an organic substance that, together with cellulose, forms the woody cell walls of plants |
| **leaf scar** | the scar left on a twig when a leaf falls off |
| **mitochondria** | a rod-shaped cell part in the cytoplasm where energy is released |
| **mitosis** | cell division that forms two new identical cells |
| **monocotyledon** | (monocot) a group of flowering plants that have seeds with one seed leaf |
| **molecule** | the smallest part of a compound that still has the chemical properties of the compound |
| **nodes** | a bud region of a stem |
| **nucleus** | the control center of the cell that directs all the cell's activities |
| **nutrients** | materials needed for plants to live |
| **organelles** | a part of the cell having a special function |
| **organism** | a living thing |
| **ovary** | the rounded, bottom part of a pistil where ovules are located; the mature ovary develops into the fruit |
| **ovule** | the parts of a flower that contain egg cells and develops into seeds |
| **palmate** | having leaflets or principal veins radiating out from a common point |
| **peduncle** | the stalk of a flower |
| **petals** | leaflike structures of flowers that surround the stamen and pistil, collectively called the corolla |
| **petiole** | the slender stalk by which a leaf blade is attached to the stem |

| | |
|---|---|
| **phloem** | the tubes that move food downward in the stem of a plant |
| **photosynthesis** | the process by which green plants use the energy from sunlight, carbon dioxide, and water to make food |
| **pinnate** | having leaflets or veins on both sides of a common axil |
| **pistil** | the female part of a plant, consisting of an ovary, style, and stigma |
| **pollen** | tiny grains from which the sperm cells of flowering plants develop |
| **pollinate** | to transfer pollen from its site of formation to a receptive surface where it may germinate |
| **protoplasm** | the living substance of which all cells are made |
| **receptacle** | the expanded tip of a peduncle to which the various parts of a flower are attached, called a flower base |
| **ribosomes** | tiny cell parts that make protein, usually found along the edge of the rough endoplasmic reticulum |
| **sepal** | green leaflike structures that surround and protect a flower bud, collectively called the calyx |
| **sperm cells** | male reproductive cells of a plant |
| **stamen** | a pollen-producing structure of a flower consisting of the filament and anther |
| **stigma** | the part of the pistil of a flowering plant that receives the pollen |
| **stomata** | openings in the epidermis of leaves through which oxygen, carbon dioxide, and water vapor enter and leave a plant |
| **style** | the stemlike part of the pistil of a flower having the stigma at its top |
| **taproot** | a large, strong root with very small side roots |
| **tissue** | a group of similar cells doing the same job |
| **transpiration** | loss of water vapor through the stomata of a leaf |
| **tuber** | a solid, thickened portion of an underground stem |
| **vacuoles** | cell parts that store food, water, and wastes |
| **venation** | the arrangement of veins in the blade of a leaf |
| **whorled** | having three or more leaves at a node |
| **xanthophylls** | a yellow pigment present in plant cells |
| **xylem** | the tubes that carry water and minerals in a plant |

# Literature List

Aliki. *Corn is Maize.* HarperCollins. New York. 1996.

Allen, Marjorie N. and Shelley Rotner. *Changes.* Simon & Schuster. New York. 1995.

Ancona, George. *Bananas: From Manolo to Margie.* Houghton Mifflin. Boston. 1990.

Anthony, Joseph. *The Dandelion Seed.* Dawn Publications. Nevada City, CA. 1997.

Back, Christine. *Bean and Plant.* Silver Burdett. Morristown, NJ. 1986.

Bash, Barbara. *Desert Giant: The World of the Saguaro Cactus.* Gibbs Smith. Layton, UT. 2002.

Bjork, Christina. *Linnea in Monet's Garden.* R & S Books. New York. 1987.

Braithwaite, Althea. *Tree (Life Cycle Books)* Longman Group USA. Chicago. 1988.

Burnie, David. *Plant (Eyewitness Books).* Dorling Kindersley. New York. 2004.

Burnie, David. *Tree (Eyewitness Books).* Dorling Kindersley. New York. 2005.

Buscaglia, Leo. *The Fall of Freddie the Leaf.* Slack, Inc. Thorofare, NJ. 1982.

Carle, Eric. *The Tiny Seed.* Simon & Schuster. New York. 2001.

Challand, Helen. *Plants Without Seeds.* Children's Press. Chicago. 1986.

Cherry, Lynne. *The Great Kapok Tree.* Harcourt (Voyager Books). San Diego. 1990.

Ehlert, Lois. *Growing Vegetable Soup.* Harcourt (Voyager Books). San Diego. 1990.

Ehlert, Lois. *Red Leaf, Yellow Leaf.* Harcourt Brace Jovanovich. San Diego. 1991.

Ehlert, Lois. *Planting a Rainbow.* Harcourt Brace Jovanovich. San Diego. 1992.

Fowler, Allan. *From Seed to Plant.* Children's Press. Chicago. 2001.

Gibbons, Gail. *The Seasons of Arnold's Apple Tree.* Harcourt. San Diego. 1998.

Haddad, Helen. *Potato Printing.* HarperCollins. New York. 1981.

Heller, Ruth. *Plants That Never Ever Bloom.* Putnam. New York. 1999.

Heller, Ruth *The Reason for a Flower.* Putnam. New York. 1999.

Hiscock, Bruce. *The Big Tree*. Boyds Mills Press. Honesdale, PA. 1999.

Howell. Laura, Kirsteen Rogers and Corinne Henderson. *World of Plants (The Usborne Internet-Linked Library of Science)*. EDC Publishing. Tulsa, OK. 2002.

Ichikawa, Satomi. *Rosy's Garden*. Putnam. New York. 1990.

Jennings, Terry. *Seeds*. Gloucester Press. New York. 1990.

Jeunesse, Gallimard and Pascale de Bourgoing. *The Tree (A First Discovery Book)*. Scholastic, Inc. New York. 1992.

Johnson, Sylvia. *Mosses*. Lerner Publications. Minneapolis. 1993.

Johnson, Sylvia. *Apple Trees*. Lerner Publications. Minneapolis. 1989.

Johnson, Sylvia. *How Leaves Change*. Lerner Publications. Minneapolis. 1986.

Johnson, Sylvia. *Potatoes*. Lerner Publications. Minneapolis. 1984.

Kellogg, Steven. *Johnny Appleseed*. HarperCollins. New York. 1988.

Kirkpatrick, Rena. *Trees*. Raintree Publishers. Milwaukee. 1985.

Lauber, Patricia. *Seeds: Pop, Stick, Glide*. Crown Books. New York. 1987.

Lerner, Carol. *Plant Families*. William Morrow. New York. 1989.

Lerner, Sharon. *I Found a Leaf*. Lerner Publications. Minneapolis. 1981.

Lottridge, Celia Barker. *The Name of the Tree*. Groundwood Books. Toronto, Ontario. 1989.

Lyon, George E. *A B Cedar: An Alphabet of Trees*. Scholastic, Inc. New York. 1996.

Mabey, Richard. *Oak and Company*. Greenwillow Books. New York. 1983.

Martin, Bill, Jr. and John Archambault. *The Ghost-Eye Tree*. Henry Holt & Co. New York. 1988.

McMillan, Bruce. *Apples How They Grow*. Houghton Mifflin. Boston. 1979.

Mitchell, Barbara. *A Pocketful of Goobers*. Lerner Publications. Minneapolis. 1991.

Overbeck, Cynthia. *How Seeds Travel*. Lerner Publications. Minneapolis. 1990.

Overbeck, Cynthia. *Sunflowers*. Lerner Publications. Minneapolis. 1981.

Overbeck, Cynthia. *Cactus*. Lerner Publications. Minneapolis. 1982.

Parnall, Peter. *Apple Tree*. Simon & Schuster. New York. 1988.

Patent, Dorothy Hinshaw. *An Apple a Day*. Dutton. New York. 1990.

Rahn, Joan. *More Plants That Changed History*. Atheneum. New York. 1985.

Rahn, Joan. *Seven Ways to Collect Plants*. Atheneum. New York. 1978.

Rahn, Joan. *Watch It Grow, Watch It Change*. Atheneum. New York. 1978.

Rockwell, Anne. *Apples and Pumpkins*. Simon & Schuster. New York. 1994.

Royston, Angela. *Life Cycle of a Sunflower*. Heinemann Library. 1998.

Ryan, Pam Munoz. *How Do You Raise a Raisin?* Charlesbridge Publishing. Watertown, MA. 2003.

Schnieper, Claudia. *An Apple Tree Through the Year*. Lerner Publications. Minneapolis. 1993.

Selsam, Millicent and Jerome Wexler. *Eat the Fruit, Plant the Seed*. William Morrow. New York. 1980.

Selsam, Millicent and Jerome Wexler. *Amazing Dandelion*. William Morrow. New York. 1987.

Silverstein, Shel. *The Giving Tree*. HarperCollins. New York. 2004 (anniversary edition).

Titherington, Jeanne. *Pumpkin, Pumpkin*. William Morrow. New York. 1990.

Tresselt, Alvin. *Autumn Harvest*. William Morrow. New York. 1991.

Tresselt, Alvin. *The Gift of the Tree*. William Morrow. New York. 1992.

Udry, Janice. *A Tree is Nice*. HarperCollins. New York. 1999.

Watts, Barrie. *Mushroom*. Silver Burdett. Morristown, NJ. 1990.

Watts, Barrie. *Potato*. Silver Burdett. Morristown, NJ. 1995.

Webster, Vera. *Plant Experiments*. Children's Press. Chicago. 1982.

Wexler, Jerome. *Flowers, Fruits, and Seeds*. Simon & Schuster. New York. 1990.

# The AIMS Program

AIMS is the acronym for "Activities Integrating Mathematics and Science." Such integration enriches learning and makes it meaningful and holistic. AIMS began as a project of Fresno Pacific University to integrate the study of mathematics and science in grades K-9, but has since expanded to include language arts, social studies, and other disciplines.

AIMS is a continuing program of the non-profit AIMS Education Foundation. It had its inception in a National Science Foundation funded program whose purpose was to explore the effectiveness of integrating mathematics and science. The project directors in cooperation with 80 elementary classroom teachers devoted two years to a thorough field-testing of the results and implications of integration.

The approach met with such positive results that the decision was made to launch a program to create instructional materials incorporating this concept. Despite the fact that thoughtful educators have long recommended an integrative approach, very little appropriate material was available in 1981 when the project began. A series of writing projects have ensued, and today the AIMS Education Foundation is committed to continue the creation of new integrated activities on a permanent basis.

The AIMS program is funded through the sale of books, products, and staff development workshops and through proceeds from the Foundation's endowment. All net income from program and products flows into a trust fund administered by the AIMS Education Foundation. Use of these funds is restricted to support of research, development, and publication of new materials. Writers donate all their rights to the Foundation to support its on-going program. No royalties are paid to the writers.

The rationale for integration lies in the fact that science, mathematics, language arts, social studies, etc., are integrally interwoven in the real world from which it follows that they should be similarly treated in the classroom where we are preparing students to live in that world. Teachers who use the AIMS program give enthusiastic endorsement to the effectiveness of this approach.

Science encompasses the art of questioning, investigating, hypothesizing, discovering, and communicating. Mathematics is the language that provides clarity, objectivity, and understanding. The language arts provide us powerful tools of communication. Many of the major contemporary societal issues stem from advancements in science and must be studied in the context of the social sciences. Therefore, it is timely that all of us take seriously a more holistic mode of educating our students. This goal motivates all who are associated with the AIMS Program. We invite you to join us in this effort.

Meaningful integration of knowledge is a major recommendation coming from the nation's professional science and mathematics associations. The American Association for the Advancement of Science in *Science for All Americans* strongly recommends the integration of mathematics, science, and technology. The National Council of Teachers of Mathematics places strong emphasis on applications of mathematics such as are found in science investigations. AIMS is fully aligned with these recommendations.

Extensive field testing of AIMS investigations confirms these beneficial results:

1. Mathematics becomes more meaningful, hence more useful, when it is applied to situations that interest students.
2. The extent to which science is studied and understood is increased, with a significant economy of time, when mathematics and science are integrated.
3. There is improved quality of learning and retention, supporting the thesis that learning which is meaningful and relevant is more effective.
4. Motivation and involvement are increased dramatically as students investigate real-world situations and participate actively in the process.

We invite you to become part of this classroom teacher movement by using an integrated approach to learning and sharing any suggestions you may have. The AIMS Program welcomes you!

© 2005 AIMS Education Foundation

# AIMS Education Foundation Programs

## Practical proven strategies to improve student achievement

When you host an AIMS workshop for elementary and middle school educators, you will know your teachers are receiving effective usable training they can apply in their classrooms immediately.

## Designed for teachers—AIMS Workshops:

- Correlate to your state standards;
- Address key topic areas, including math content, science content, problem solving, and process skills;
- Teach you how to use AIMS' effective hands-on approach;
- Provide practice of activity-based teaching;
- Address classroom management issues, higher-order thinking skills, and materials;
- Give you AIMS resources; and
- Offer college (graduate-level) credits for many courses.

## Aligned to district and administrator needs—AIMS workshops offer:

- Flexible scheduling and grade span options;
- Custom (one-, two-, or three-day) workshops to meet specific schedule, topic and grade-span needs;
- Pre-packaged one-day workshops on most major topics—only $3,900 for up to 30 participants (includes all materials and expenses);
- Prepackaged *week-long* workshops (four- or five-day formats) for in-depth math and science training—only $12,300 for up to 30 participants (includes all materials and expenses);
- Sustained staff development, by scheduling workshops throughout the school year and including follow-up and assessment;
- Eligibility for funding under the Eisenhower Act and No Child Left Behind; and
- Affordable professional development—save when you schedule consecutive-day workshops.

## University Credit—Correspondence Courses

AIMS offers correspondence courses through a partnership with Fresno Pacific University.

- Convenient distance-learning courses—you study at your own pace and schedule. No computer or Internet access required!

The tuition for each three-semester unit graduate-level course is $264 plus a materials fee.

## The AIMS Instructional Leadership Program

This is an AIMS staff-development program seeking to prepare facilitators for leadership roles in science/math education in their home districts or regions. Upon successful completion of the program, trained facilitators become members of the AIMS Instructional Leadership Network, qualified to conduct AIMS workshops, teach AIMS in-service courses for college credit, and serve as AIMS consultants. Intensive training is provided in mathematics, science, process and thinking skills, workshop management, and other relevant topics.

## Introducing AIMS Science Core Curriculum

Developed in alignment with your state standards, AIMS' Science Core Curriculum gives students the opportunity to build content knowledge, thinking skills, and fundamental science processes.

- *Each* grade specific module has been developed to extend the AIMS approach to full-year science programs.
- *Each* standards-based module includes math, reading, hands-on investigations, and assessments.

Like all AIMS resources these core modules are able to serve students at all stages of readiness, making these a great value across the grades served in your school.

**For current information regarding the programs described above, please complete the following:**

---

### *Information Request*

Please send current information on the items checked:

____ *Basic Information Packet* on AIMS materials ____ Hosting information for AIMS workshops
____ *AIMS Instructional Leadership Program* ____ AIMS Science Core Curriculum

Name _____ Phone _____

Address_____
          Street                                      City                         State          Zip

---

© 2005 AIMS Education Foundation

## Magazine

YOUR K-9 MATH AND SCIENCE
CLASSROOM ACTIVITIES RESOURCE

The AIMS Magazine is your source for standards-based, hands-on math and science investigations. Each issue is filled with teacher-friendly, ready-to-use activities that engage students in meaningful learning.

• *Four issues each year (fall, winter, spring, and summer).*

**Current issue is shipped with all past issues within that volume.**

| 1820 | Volume XX | 2005-2006 | $19.95 |
| 1821 | Volume XXI | 2006-2007 | $19.95 |
| Two-Volume Combination | | | |
| M20507 | Volumes XX & XXI | 2005-2007 | $34.95 |

**Back Volumes Available**
**Complete volumes available for purchase:**

| 1802 | Volume II | 1987-1988 | $19.95 |
| 1804 | Volume IV | 1989-1990 | $19.95 |
| 1805 | Volume V | 1990-1991 | $19.95 |
| 1807 | Volume VII | 1992-1993 | $19.95 |
| 1808 | Volume VIII | 1993-1994 | $19.95 |
| 1809 | Volume IX | 1994-1995 | $19.95 |
| 1810 | Volume X | 1995-1996 | $19.95 |
| 1811 | Volume XI | 1996-1997 | $19.95 |
| 1812 | Volume XII | 1997-1998 | $19.95 |
| 1813 | Volume XIII | 1998-1999 | $19.95 |
| 1814 | Volume XIV | 1999-2000 | $19.95 |
| 1815 | Volume XV | 2000-2001 | $19.95 |
| 1816 | Volume XVI | 2001-2002 | $19.95 |
| 1817 | Volume XVII | 2002-2003 | $19.95 |
| 1818 | Volume XVIII | 2003-2004 | $19.95 |
| 1819 | Volume XIX | 2004-2005 | $35.00 |

Call today to order back volumes: 1.888.733.2467.

## Call **1.888.733.2467** or go to **www.aimsedu.org**

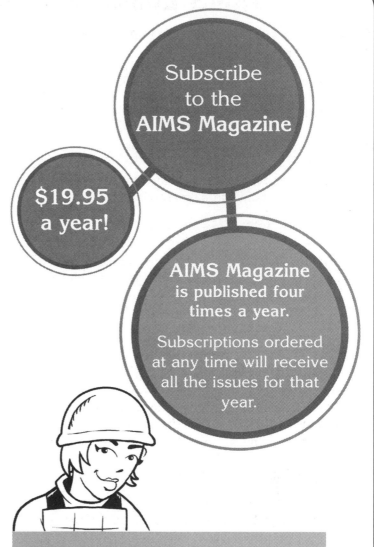

### Subscribe to the AIMS Magazine

**$19.95 a year!**

**AIMS Magazine** is published four times a year.

Subscriptions ordered at any time will receive all the issues for that year.

### AIMS Online – www.aimsedu.org

For the latest on AIMS publications, tips, information, and promotional offers, check out AIMS on the web at www.aimsedu.org. Explore our activities, database, discover featured activities, and get information on our college courses and workshops, too.

**AIMS News**
While visiting the AIMS website, sign up for AIMS News, our FREE e-mail newsletter. Published semi-monthly, AIMS News brings you food for thought and subscriber-only savings and specials. Each issue delivers:

• **Thought-provoking articles on curriculum and pedagogy;**
• **Information about our newest books and products; and**
• **Sample activities.**

**Sign up today!**

© 2005 AIMS Education Foundation

# AIMS Program Publications

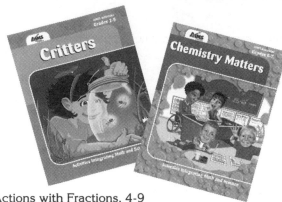

Actions with Fractions, 4-9
Awesome Addition and Super Subtraction, 2-3
Bats Incredible! 2-4
Brick Layers II, 4-9
Chemistry Matters, 4-7
Counting on Coins, K-2
Cycles of Knowing and Growing, 1-3
Crazy about Cotton, 3-7
Critters, 2-5
Down to Earth, 5-9
Electrical Connections, 4-9
Exploring Environments, K-6
Fabulous Fractions, 3-6
Fall into Math and Science, K-1
Field Detectives, 3-6
Finding Your Bearings, 4-9
Floaters and Sinkers, 5-9
From Head to Toe, 5-9
Fun with Foods, 5-9
Glide into Winter with Math & Science, K-1
Gravity Rules! 5-12
Hardhatting in a Geo-World, 3-5
It's About Time, K-2
It Must Be A Bird, Pre-K-2
Jaw Breakers and Heart Thumpers, 3-5
Looking at Geometry, 6-9
Looking at Lines, 6-9
Machine Shop, 5-9
Magnificent Microworld Adventures, 5-9
Marvelous Multiplication and Dazzling Division, 4-5
Math + Science, A Solution, 5-9
Mostly Magnets, 2-8
Movie Math Mania, 6-9
Multiplication the Algebra Way, 4-8
Off the Wall Science, 3-9
Our Wonderful World, 5-9
Out of This World, 4-8
Overhead and Underfoot, 3-5
Paper Square Geometry:
    The Mathematics of Origami, 5-12
Puzzle Play, 4-8
Pieces and Patterns, 5-9
Popping With Power, 3-5
Positive vs. Negative, 6-9

Primarily Bears, K-6
Primarily Earth, K-3
Primarily Physics, K-3
Primarily Plants, K-3
Problem Solving: Just for the Fun of It! 4-9
Proportional Reasoning, 6-9
Ray's Reflections, 4-8
Sense-Able Science, K-1
Soap Films and Bubbles, 4-9
Solve It! K-1: Problem-Solving Strategies, K-1
Solve It! 2nd: Problem-Solving Strategies, 2
Spatial Visualization, 4-9
Spills and Ripples, 5-12
Spring into Math and Science, K-1
The Amazing Circle, 4-9
The Budding Botanist, 3-6
The Sky's the Limit, 5-9
Through the Eyes of the Explorers, 5-9
Under Construction, K-2
Water Precious Water, 2-6
Weather Sense: Temperature, Air Pressure, and Wind, 4-5
Weather Sense: Moisture, 4-5
Winter Wonders, K-2

**Spanish/English Editions***
Brinca de alegria hacia la Primavera con las
    Matemáticas y Ciencias, K-1
Cáete de gusto hacia el Otoño con las
    Matemáticas y Ciencias, K-1
Conexiones Eléctricas, 4-9
El Botanista Principiante, 3-6
Los Cinco Sentidos, K-1
Ositos Nada Más, K-6
Patine al Invierno con Matemáticas y Ciencias, K-1
Piezas y Diseños, 5-9
Primariamente Física, K-3
Primariamente Plantas, K-3
Principalmente Imanes, 2-8

\*   All Spanish/English Editions include student pages in Spanish and
    teacher and student pages in English.

**Spanish Edition**
Constructores II: Ingeniería Creativa Con Construcciones
    LEGO® 4-9
    The entire book is written in Spanish. English pages not included.

**Other Science and Math Publications**
Historical Connections in Mathematics, Vol. I, 5-9
Historical Connections in Mathematics, Vol. II, 5-9
Historical Connections in Mathematics, Vol. III, 5-9
Mathematicians are People, Too
Mathematicians are People, Too, Vol. II
What's Next, Volume 1, 4-12
What's Next, Volume 2, 4-12
What's Next, Volume 3, 4-12

For further information write to:
AIMS Education Foundation • P.O. Box 8120 • Fresno, California 93747-8120
www.aimsedu.org • Fax 559.255.6396

© 2005 AIMS Education Foundation

# Duplication Rights

**Standard Duplication Rights**

Purchasers of AIMS activities (individually or in books and magazines) may make up to 200 copies of any portion of the purchased activities, provided these copies will be used for educational purposes and only at one school site.

Workshop or conference presenters may make one copy of a purchased activity for each participant, with a limit of five activities per workshop or conference session.

Standard duplication rights apply to activities received at workshops, free sample activities provided by AIMS, and activities received by conference participants.

All copies must bear the AIMS Education Foundation copyright information.

---

**Unlimited Duplication Rights**

To ensure compliance with copyright regulations, AIMS users may upgrade from standard to unlimited duplication rights. Such rights permit unlimited duplication of purchased activities (including revisions) for use at a given school site.

Activities received at workshops are eligible for upgrade from standard to unlimited duplication rights.

Free sample activities and activities received as a conference participant are not eligible for upgrade from standard to unlimited duplication rights.

---

**Upgrade Fees**

The fees for upgrading from standard to unlimited duplication rights are:
- $5 per activity per site; and
- $25 per book per site;
- $10 per magazine issue per site.

The cost of upgrading is shown in the following examples:
- activity: 5 activities x 5 sites x $5 = $125
- book: 10 books x 5 sites x $25 = $1250
- magazine issue: 1 issue x 5 sites x $10 = $50

---

**Purchasing Unlimited Duplication Rights**

To purchase unlimited duplication rights, please provide us the following:
1. The name of the individual responsible for coordinating the purchase of duplication rights.
2. The title of each book, activity, and magazine issue to be covered.
3. The number of school sites and name of each site for which rights are being purchased.
4. Payment (check, purchase order, credit card)

Requested duplication rights are automatically authorized with payment. The individual responsible for coordinating the purchase of duplication rights will be sent a certificate verifying the purchase.

---

**Internet Use**

Permission to make AIMS activities available on the Internet is determined on a case-by-case basis.

- P. O. Box 8120, Fresno, CA 93747-8120 •
- aimsed@aimsedu.org • www.aimsedu.org •
- 559.255.6396 (fax) • 888.733.2467 (toll free) •

© 2005 AIMS Education Foundation

# DATE DUE

ILL#86500436 FTU 02/28/2012

ILL#10852745 FTU 10/11/13

Demco, Inc. 38-293

Flagler College Library
P.O. Box 1027
St. Augustine, FL 32085